A BUDDHIST GUIDE TO THE POWER PLACES OF THE KATHMANDU VALLEY

A BUDDHIST GUIDE TO THE POWER PLACES OF THE KATHMANDU VALLEY

Keith Dowman

Published and Distributed 2018 by
Vajra Books
Jyatha, Thamel, P.O. Box 21779, Kathmandu, Nepal
Tel.: 977-1-4220562, Fax: 977-1-4246536
e-mail: bidur_la@mos.com.np
www.vajrabooks.com.np

Cover Painting: Bipin Raj Shrestha

ISBN 978-9937-506-02-1

Printed in Nepal

LAMA THUBTEN ZOPA RINPOCHE

SPIRITUAL DIRECTOR
Foundation for the Preservation of the Mahayana Tradition

Message

Why we need to meditate is simply because we want happiness and we don't want suffering. Even with external phenomena each has their own cause. For example, chillie comes from its own cause - it's own seed, something which is hot so the result is hot, while raisins come from a seed which is sweet. Put another way, chillie doesn't come from the seed of the raisin, which is sweet, and raisins don't come from chillies, which are hot. Raisins come from raisin seeds and chillies come from chillie seeds.

Just as raisins come from sweet raisin seeds, and chillies come from hot chillie seeds, like that, happiness doesn't come from non-virtue. The non-virtuous attitude is ignorant of Dharma and karma, ignorant of what is right and what brings happiness to oneself and to others and ignorant of what is wrong and brings harm to oneself and others. Anger and attachment are also non-virtuous and their grasping destroys happiness as does the actions motivated by them. That's why these actions become non-virtue and result only in suffering. Suffering doesn't come from virtue or the pure thoughts of non-anger, non-ignorance, non-attachment. The actions motivated by pure thoughts are transformed into virtuous actions and their results are only happiness. The second Buddha, the Savior Nagajuna, the great Indian scholar and highly attained-one said, 'Actions born from ignorance, anger and attachment are non-virtuous and from that all the sufferings of migratory beings arise. The actions born from non-anger, non- attachment and non-ignorance are virtuous and all the happiness of transmigratory

1632 SE 11th Avenue • Portland, OR 97214 USA
Tel: 1 (503) 808-1588 • Fax: 1 (408) 516-9850 • roger@fpmt.org • www.FPMT.org

beings arises from them. So then happiness and suffering have totally separate evolutions.

All one's happiness and suffering come from one's mind but from different kinds of minds. When a root is poisonous, the stem, leaves, flowers and fruit - everything is poisonous. If a root is medicinal, then the trunk, etc. - everything is medicinal. From the impure mind, the distorted, obscured mind comes samsara - all the oceans of human beings' sufferings, the oceans of devas of the form and formless realms' sufferings and no question about desire realm sufferings. This includes not only human beings' suffering but the sufferings of devas of the desire realms and the sufferings of the lower realms -oceans of human, oceans of animal, oceans of lower realm sufferings and not only that, future lives' sufferings. As it is mentioned in the Bodhisattvacharyavatara by the great Indian saint Shantideva, 'Who created the hot burning iron ground of the hell realm?' It is said by Buddha, that it is created by the evil mind, the evil mind being the non-virtuous thought.

Even the problems of this life, such as the unhappiness and depression when disappointed, due to not achieving something, come from the non-virtuous thought because of desire clinging to the pleasures of this life. Liking the happiness and comfort of this life and disliking unhappiness and discomfort are both non-virtuous thoughts. So this life can be in this, or opposite the worldly attitude, the non-virtuous thought. Without opposing the worldly attitude, life is suffering, like the experiences of attachment, desire and clinging, and the feeling of comfort when there's happiness, praise, reputation and material receiving and the dislike when these four things don't happen. In all these ways it's life with suffering, with no inner peace in one's heart. The life is always up and down, with no stability and one can never get satisfaction. As Buddha said in a sutra 'As far as one follows desire, one can't get satisfaction." So it is similar to in the song sung by the Rolling Stones, 'I tried and I tried but I can't get no satisfaction.' What drives life crazy leads to so much unhappiness and dissatisfaction. To fulfill this life's desire, one engages in killing, stealing, sexual misconduct and sexual abuse, lies and slander, divisive speech, ill-will, covetness and heresy - many non-virtuous actions that harm others, many sentient beings.

These actions harm not just oneself and family members but 100's, 1000's and millions of people in the country and in the world. As shown by history, many beings have been killed in the world by just one person who didn't take care of and subdue their mind. They didn't make their mind

Dharma, didn't make it virtuous and especially didn't generate contentment or renunciation and, moreover, didn't generate compassion towards other sentient beings. Compassion is the peaceful happy mind, possessing patience. Instead they followed negative thoughts, beginning less self-cherishing thoughts of desire, which all came from ignorance and created so many enemies for themselves, obliging so many people in this world to become an enemy for them. Here there is a clear connection to the selfish mind. One's own negative mind makes all the enemies for oneself in this world and destroys the happiness of millions and millions of sentient beings.

What makes the mind transform into Dharma, to transform from selfishness to the kind heart cherishing others, from anger to patience which then becomes happiness for oneself, the family and the world, becoming a peaceful, happy mind of contentment, which stops giving harm, suffering and problems to the family and sentient beings and instead gives peace and happiness to the family and to sentient beings, all living beings, through the power of positive thoughts? One person who was previously the opposite, harming millions of people with a negative mind, lacking Dharma practice, can transform their mind into pure thoughts and becomes peaceful and happy, bringing so much sun-shining peace and happiness in the country and the world, life to life, to all sentient beings.

There's an urgency, an emergency, to do this right away. The mind must become Dharma. This is what makes us meditate. Making the mind familiar with positive thoughts is meditation. People might think that one doesn't need to be a spiritual person, that someone outside might need to become spiritual but oneself doesn't need to practise meditation and be a spiritual person. This is totally wrong. Since what you want is happiness, this is totally wrong. Transforming the mind into Dharma is meditation. What is called real meditation means training in having a virtuous mind. Training in non-virtue - in ignorance, anger and attachment - is not needed. Doing a meditation retreat with such negative thoughts being generated, is not meditation. One is doing something wrong, something is missing. Through correct meditation, training of the mind in virtue, one has less thought of self and more thought about others and a less painful mind of desire and more inner peace.

Everyone wants this - inner peace and happiness, so we can see very clearly that everyone has to practice, everyone needs meditation. Nobody wants to die, get sick or become old. Everyone wants to be young. But there is no choice. We have to go through what is the nature of life - moment by moment getting older and going towards death. In Tibetan, this is *dro.wa* - one who is going. Another meaning is transmigrating under the power of karma and delusion without the slightest freedom.

Therefore if one doesn't like these things, one needs the wisdom that our kind Buddha revealed, that suffering comes from the causes of karma and delusion and that these causes can be ceased. How? By actualizing the path. Buddha revealed that there's a path to the sorrow less state beyond suffering. These ideas are just fundamental Buddhist ideas, not introducing the Mahayana path, such as the five paths and the ten bhumis - the universal vehicle which takes universal responsibility to attain full enlightenment for sentient beings. These ideas also don't introduce what is also from the great vehicle, the secret mantra vajrayana Mahayana great vehicle, the means to achieve enlightenment more quickly, without the need to collect merit for 3 countless great eons, but instead to collect all the merits in this life in order to become enlightened quickly in this life. That's one purpose to practice the great vehicle vajrayana. What I'm saying is, there is the need, without choice, to learn Buddha Dharma and practice, to meditate and actualize all the path. If one likes suffering, rebirth, death, old age, sickness - all these sufferings, one doesn't need to learn Dharma.

So now, here, the purpose of holy places existing is to help the mind, to support and bless the mind which is the root of samsara and nirvana, hell and enlightenment. Holy places help the mind to transform into the path to liberation and enlightenment which requires generating useful faith and wisdom from which you receive blessings of the Guru, Buddha, Dharma and Sangha - those great saints who had attainment in those places and from the places one then receives blessings.

The purpose of making pilgrimage is to purify the mind of negative karma and its imprints and to collect merit while making prayers to bless the heart, the mind. The places of the enlightened beings, the Buddhas and the bodhisattvas have blessings and when one goes to the holy places, the holy beings bless us the ordinary beings. They bless one's heart. So we go there to receive blessings.

So it is very important to learn Dharma, and also to understand the real meaning of holy places and pilgrimage. It is possible, as a tourist, with no Dharma understanding or devotion to visit holy places and get a 'click' of devotion. For some people, it's possible. It's their karma. But generally, pilgrimage is done with a mind of faith and Dharma understanding and then blessings are received according to one's faith. It is important to preserve holy places, in order that beings can purify, accumulate and achieve enlightenment, through purifying their oceans of samsaric sufferings. For doing this, thank you very much.

We get more faith the more we understand the path to enlightenment, the qualities of the Sangha and especially Buddha and the more understanding we have of the holy places and the attainments of those yogis who practiced there, understanding that what they did was not easy, taking 100's of lifetimes, eons, to collect merit and practise. For example, Buddha's relics are the result of three countless great eons practise of charity, giving His life for sentient beings, practicing pure morality, patience, perseverance, concentration and so forth and practicing for all of us, all sentient beings, collecting the two accumulations of wisdom and compassion to achieve Dharmakaya and Rupakaya. We can't see Buddha, but we can see relics, which have the power to lead us to enlightenment. Similarly, we should understand how precious the holy places are.

Thank you very much.

HIMALAYAN BUDDHIST MEDITATION CENTRE
Akanistha Guest House
Founders
Lama ThuptenYeshe
Lama Thupten Zopa Rinpoche
Spiritual Director
Lama Thupten Zopa Rinpoche

Foreword

I left the Kathmandu valley with all its secrets, about 20 years ago and I have just came back to find that one of those hidden treasures is still unearthed.

I phoned my friend Keith Dowman, a scholar and author of some extraordinary texts, who I have not seen for the last 25 years. We talked about the possibility of bringing this treasure to light, and the response against all the odds was affirmative.

This brief telephone conversation happened just an hour before Keith was leaving the country to Varanasi, of all places. We met at Tribhuvan International Airport, Kathmandu where we decided to unravel "A Buddhist Guide to the Power Places of the Kathmandu Valley" a research paper written by him in the 70s, and only published once or twice in the 80s.

This took place three weeks ago, just one week after Kyabje Lama Zopa Rinpoche, accepted Himalayan Buddhist Meditation Center's invitation to give a Public Talk in Kathmandu, during his brief visit to Kopan Monastery.

The idea to give an enlightened presentation on the value of meditation and pilgrimage, together with the launch of a hidden pilgrimage guide book, caught momentum when Nepal Tourism Board and Himalayan Buddhist Meditation Center decided to go for collaborative promotions to highlight spiritual heritage of Nepal to a wider audience.

This book and the Public Talk are the fruits of this collaboration and the fruition of many karmas of the past. My wife Tanya, was just telling me, while she was copyediting the manuscript, that the story of the hunter, the dear and the dog, in the Milarepa thangka that Lama Thubten Zopa

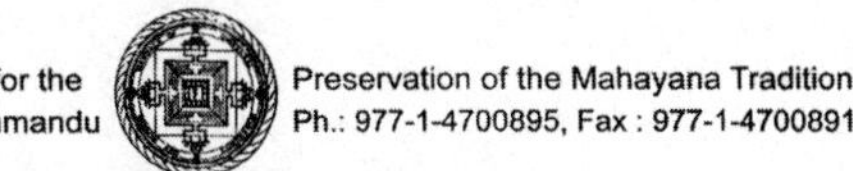

Member of the Foundation for the Preservation of the Mahayana Tradition
P.O.Box 5761, Thamel,Kathmandu Ph.: 977-1-4700895, Fax : 977-1-4700891

Rinpoche instructed me to paint a few years ago, and which is hanging in front of me at this very moment in time, actually happened in one of the power places mentioned in this book; No 47 Nyishang Kurti, near Bhaktapur.

Sarva Mangalam!

Antonio Pascual
Spiritual Program Coordinator
Himalayan Buddhist Meditation Center
Kathmandu, Thamel, Nepal
10 December 2007

Contents

A Buddhist Guide to the Power Places of the Kathmandu Valley

Precious symbols of the Minds of the Conquering Buddhas of the Ten
Directions,
Swayambhunath, Boudhnath and Namo Buddha,
We pray to you from the innermost depths of our hearts.
With an all-embracing relationship with these three supreme symbols,
All adversity, troubles and obstacles are removed,
All our wishes are actually fulfilled,
And ultimately we cross the ocean of samsara with all other beings.
By the grace of these three stupas may we attain the level of the Four
Buddha Modes.

This is a guide for all pilgrims to the Valley of Kathmandu, for both the eminent and the lowly.

1. KIMDOL VIHARA

When you travel the road to India from Tibet you will first come to Vulture Peak Monastery (Bya-rgod phung-po-ri'i dgon-pa, Gridhrakuta Vihara). You can honour the chief image of the monastery, Munindra, visit the Avalokitesvara fasting room (smyung gnas lha-khang) on the first floor, the Maitreya Temple on the north side, and other images in the neighbourhood, the chief of which is the image of the Buddha in parinirvana posture.

"In the neighbourhood of [Ri-bo `Bigs-byed] is a hill called Vulture Peak, and it is said that this is the place where a thousand Buddhas of the bhadrakalpa first generated enlightened mind, and where the woman Jadzima (Bya-rdzi-ma), who built the stupa at Boudha, attained Buddhahood." (bLa-ma bTsan-po)

"To the southwest of Swayambhu is Vulture Peak... Then 21,000 arhats from Vulture Peak took earth and deposited it beneath the dome of the Stupa." (Shing-kun dkar-chag) Previously the Swayambhu Stupa had been resting upon a wooden axis pole and four stone pillars founded on the Valley floor. But the Swayambhu Purana has a different idea [see Manjusri Hill].

The Tibetans call the Kimdol Hill, south of Swayambhu, Vulture Peak, which is the name of the hill in India where Sakyamuni delivered the Prajnaparamita sutras. The Newars call it Kimdo, which means 'Heap of Rice' ('bras-spungs) in Newari. (Chos-kyi Nyi-ma)

In front of the gate of the Vihara, which is considered pre- eminent in Kathmandu (i.e. in the 18th century), is a sacred bodhi tree (bodhivrksa). Many Lamas have stayed in this Vihara, among them, the (13th) Karmapa, the (10th) Zhamarpa, (the 6th) Drukpa Rinpoche, (the 8th) Situ, (Kathog) Rig-'dzin-chen-po, and others. (Chos-kyi Nyi-ma)

All these Lamas visiting Nepal and staying in Kimdol Vihara were contemporaries of Chos-kyi Nyi-ma. The 10th Zhamarpa (1742-1792), who made the disastrous treaty with King Rana Bahadur Shah in 1789, after Tibetan forces had been beaten at the border and was then forced to remain in exile after his monasteries had been seized, his Hat buried and the Zhamarpa line declared defunct, assisted in the major reconstruction of Swayambhu with the 13th Karmapa (1733-1797) and their teacher, the rNying-ma-pa Ka-thog-Rig-' dzin-chen-po Tse-dbang Nor-bu (1698-1755). This major repair of work on the garbhapita, (the Stupa's bowl) and also on the environs of the Stupa was finished in 1750. The 8th Situ (1700-1774), who had come to Nepal much earlier in the century (ca. 1723) with his own generation of young tulkus on an adventurous pilgrimage (the 12th Karmapa, 1703-1732, and the 8th Zhamarpa, 1695-1732, who had been born in Yol-mo), was known as Kun-mkhyen Situ or Situ Pan-chen. He stayed on in the Valley and later returned, gaining a reputation among Saivites and Buddhists alike as a great debater and scholar who translated a short version of the Swayambhu Purana, as well as other Sanskrit works into Tibetan. Like Ka-thog-pa, he was a Guru of the younger visitors. The 13th Karmapa, bDud-`dul rdo-rje, was received with honour and elephants by Jaya Prakas Malla (reigned 1722-1768), just as Jagajjaya Malla (reigned 1722-1736) had received his young predecessor who, according to his biography, was feted and given a week's royal hospitality, perhaps in return for saving Nepal by magic from the plague and drought which caused many deaths in 1723. In Namo Buddha, the King of Bhaktapur, Ranajit Malla, also received him with elephants. In the preceding century the 6th Zhamarpa (1564-1630) had patronised the construction of four golden altars in the four cardinal directions of the Swayambhu Stupa. An inscription of Sivasimha commemorates the consecration in 1614. We do not know where these earlier visitors stayed, but we do know of Rang-rig-ras-pa's association with the Vihara in the late 17th century, and also of the writer of the Swayambhu Chronicles' residence there. It appears that Kimdol Vihara was virtually a bKa'-brgyud-pa establishment in the 17th and 18th centuries. A thorough reading of the biographies of all these bKa'-brgyud Lamas and of Ka-thog Rig-'dzin-chen-po would prove most revealing. (See Douglas and White)

Sakyamuni Buddha is the principal image in the ground floor shrine room of Kimdol Vihara. In the first floor shrine room, where the abbess of the nunnery presides, is an image of a thousand-armed Avalokitesvara (Mahakarunika). Maitreya is the main image in the nani-bahal immediately to the north, and a little further down the hill northwards is the temple containing the parinirvana Buddha image.

2. SWAYAMBHU STUPA

'Phags-pa shing-kun (Sublime Trees): Swayambhu (Self-sprung): near Kimdol (sKyim-grol) = 'Liberating Draught') is Swayambhu. On top of a jewel lotus blessed by the Buddha Vipaswi (gNam-par-gzigs), the Jina Vajradhara spontaneously arose from the Pure Land of Akanistha as a great sacred Tree of Life (mChod-sdong chen-po – a Bodhi Tree or stupa) called Jnana Gandola Swayambhu (The Self-Sprung Temple of Wisdom) which brings spiritual release by sight of it, hearing of it, reflecting upon it, or touching it. Look into Newar chronicles called the Swayambhu Purana for extensive details on the arising of thirteen billion times more merit (for practising mantra etc.) in this place than in other great power places, and other interesting topics.

Shing-kun dkar-chag relates fragments of the prophecies made by Sakyamuni in the Gosrnga-vyakarana-sutra (gLang-ru lung-bstan-gyi mdo) concerning the origin of the stupa Goma Salagandha, which is usually confused with the Swayambhu Stupa by Tibetans of today. As with the Manjushri-mulatantra, the Tibetans have interpreted prophecies which concerned another country to concern themselves. "When the Buddha was living in Vaisali he prophesied in this manner to Sariputra and Ananda: 'Hereafter, a town called Kusala (dGe-ba), or Li-yul, will arise on the frontiers of India. In the Gamodeva Lake is the Ox-horn Prophecy Mountain (Gosrnga Vyakarana Parvata), and in the Gomadeva Lake the Goma Salagandha Stupa will arise. In the middle of the lake will be a thousand petalled lotus, and in the centre of the lotus will be an image of Sakyamuni, while on the petals will be a thousand Bodhisattvas of the Tenth Grade.' Then Sariputra, the chief of the Buddha's retinue, asked him, 'What will be the cause of such an eventuality?' And the Buddha replied, 'The cause will be the thousand emanations consequent upon my parinirvana'." (Shing-kun dkar-chag)

The sceptical Lama bTsan-po says, "It is generally believed that [the Swayambhu Stupa] is the Goma Salagandha Stupa that is mentioned in the Gosrnga-vyakarana-sutra (The Ox-Horn Prophecy Sutra), and that it enshrines the relics of Kasyapa; but since Goma Salagandha is in Khotan (Li-yul) and the relics of Kasyapa are in India, it is difficult to believe these stories. However, the Stupa gives immense blessings. (bLa-ma bTsan-po) Chos-kyi Nyi-ma is even more scathing about such Tibetan beliefs.

Concerning the origin of the Tibetan name Shing-kun for Swayambhu: "Then after 21,000 arhats from Vulture Peak had taken earth and piled it beneath the dome of the Stupa, Nagarjuna cut off his hair and scattered it about, praying, 'May all kinds of trees grow on this sublime Stupa!' And after many species of tree had grown tall around the Stupa, it became known as 'Sublime Trees' ('Phags-pa Shing-kun). (Shing-kun dkar-chag) But it is most likely that since the Stupa arose spontaneously at the time of the Buddha Sikhi (gTsug-gtor-can) and became known as Swayambhu (Self-Sprung), and that since the old Newar rendering was Sihmanggu, currently Singgu (i.e. in the 18th century), the Tibetan Shing-kun is a corruption of the Newari name. (Chos-kyi Nyi-ma)

Shing-kun dkar-chag describes the Stupa like this: "Beneath the Stupa of Swayambhu is a place of the Nagas. About that is a live turtle, and upon the back of the turtle stands the Tree of Life axis (tshogs-shing) which is 7 fathoms (42') in circumference at its root and 42 fathoms (252') in height. In the western lattice of the axis are the self-manifest 5,408 gods. In the cardinal directions are one Magadha measure of the relics of the jina Sakyamuni. The skin of the King Suvarnavarman (gSer-gyi Go-cha), upon which is depicted the mandala of Samvara and the 62 gods, is to be found therein. It is said that the outer, inner and secret fields of synchronicity can be devined there from…"

"When the Buddha Sakyamuni was alive, King Suvarnavarman (gSer-gyi Go-cha) was [the Stupa's] patron. (Shing-kun dkar-chag) No king with a name like this can be found in the lists of Newar chronicles. Perhaps the name is derived from the Manjusri-mulatantra.

There appears to be more references to the Swayambhu Stupa than any other power place in the Valley in the annals of all Tibetan sects except the rNying-ma-pa. For example, regarding the annals of the Ma-gcig Zha-ma lineage, this great yogini's brother `Khong-bu-pa (1069-1144), – one of many Tibetan scholar-yogins to come to Nepal during the phyi-dar, the second spreading of the doctrine – took instruction from Pham-thing-pa, Ye-rang-pa (the Patan walla) and the Bengali Atulyavajra, who were Nepal's finest teachers of that day. He had his mortal remains brought to Nepal with those of his sister by his son, Khong-gsar-pa, who had them consecrated by his Guru Jayasena. This Khang-gsar-pa had "the parasol hoisted above the Swayambhu caitya on numerous occasions" and "gathered about him many yoginis and ascetic yogins who were residents of Swayambhu and performed ganacakras on many occasions." (Blue Annals) The Saivites were flourishing at this time, and like the great translator Rwa-lo, the Tibetans fought many magical battles with them, although, according to the Tibetan chronicles, the Buddhists were inevitably victorious. (Blue Annals) Atisa, used a pilgrimage to Swayambhu as an excuse to leave Vikramasila Monastery in Bengal and escape from his students, – who would have preferred that he stayed, - so that he could run across the border to Tibet to expiate his jealousy of the monastic tradition by reforming and purifying Tibetan monasticism.

The Abbot Atisa had given his ex-Guru, the yogin Maitripa, a room at his monastery of Vikramasila, and later was astonished to discover that Maitripa had been performing puja with meat and wine within the monastery's confines. Atisa asked him to leave, whereupon with a sniff Maitripa took up his bed and walked off through a wall. Later, Atisa apologised to Maitripa who told him that the way to expiate his sin was to go to Tibet and reform Tibetan monasticism. (But see Alaka Chattopadhyaya p.134)

Our basic guide describes the origin of the Stupa very simply and concisely. Adapting the metaphor of the Swayambhu Purana, Ngag-dbang rDo-rje mentions Buddha Vipaswi who threw the seed of the original thousand-petalled lotus into Lake Nag Hrad during the satya or kritya-yuga, and he mentions the jewel, the ruby (padmaraga), that was at the centre of the lotus, diffusing the great light that pervaded the world. The jina Vajradhara is the anthropomorphic representation of the dharmadhatu that is self-arisen and self-existent. He arises as the Stupa out of Akanistha ('Og-min), the pure land of the dharmakaya, the dharmadhatu as paradise here and now. The Bodhi Tree, the Tree of life, the Stupa, these are all symbolic variations upon the same theme. The gandola is the form of the stupa and wisdom (jnana, ye-shes) is its nature.

The Tibetan sources give some historical clues concerning the foundation and history of restoration of the Stupa. If we accept Santikar Acarya as the actual builder of the concrete Stupa and accept Shing-kun dkar-chag's assertion that Amsuvarman was Santikar's contemporary, since Amsuvarman reigned between 576 and 615 - the Stupa dates from the early 7th century. But because Santikar is associated with the establishment of the vajrayana this date assumes a very early arrival of Tantra in Nepal. There is only one early inscription at Swayambhu, and we have only incidental literary eseence that the Stupa was worshipped by countless devotees from all over the Buddhist world, among them some of the most famous names in Buddhist history: Nagarjuna, Santideva, Naropa, Vagisvarakirti, Savari, Jalandharipa, Padmasambhava et al.

Undoubtedly, between the 7th and 14th centuries the structure was restored many times, as earthquakes assure that no building in the Valley can survive for even a century without attention However, the first evidence of restoration informs us that the damage just repaired was not caused by nature but by man. An inscription records the ravages of the Muslim Shams Ud-din's armies in 1349 and that the principal patron of the repair work was a certain minister, Saktimalla Bhalloka. We identify him as the Ba'-ro (Bhalloka-Bhallo-Bharo-'Ba'-ro – which was an honorific title) of Shing-kun dkar-chag. He was assisted by governor (dpon-chen) Sakya-bzang-po, who was perhaps a scion of the `Khon of Sa-skya, a Tibetan scholar (dbU-gTsang dGe-shes) and Lama dbU-pa. The 'axis' of the stupa was replaced at this time. Then in 1505, during another major restoration, which Yol-mo-pa Sakya bZang-po patronised, the wheel and pinnacle were placed on top by gTsang-smyon, the crazy yogin Sangs-rygas rGyal-mtshan from West Tibet. The 6th Zhamarpa had the four gilt shrines placed at the cardinal directions in 1614. Rang-rig-ras-pa had a new pinnacle (ganjira) erected during the reign of Parthivendra Malla, the consecration taking place in 1694. The next major restoration was consecrated in 1750, probably in the wake of an earthquake, as the extensive restoration included the environs of the Stupa. Ka-thog Rig-

'dzin-chen-po, the 13th Karmapa and Situ Pan-chen were the patrons of this restoration. The Tibetan inscription on the pillar on the southeast side of the Stupa commemorates this event. Shing-kun dkar-chag would mention only names that have meaning for the writer's Tibetan readers and we should not assume that the Stupa has been kept in repair through the devotion and wealth of the Tibetans alone. Both Saivites and Vaisnavas, kings and commoners, have paid homage to the Stupa down the centuries, and we can be certain that without a king's permission and support nothing could have been achieved. I have no date on the history of the Stupa since 1750 except to note that in the past decade attempts to shore upon the eastern flank of the hill have failed, and unless the most recent undertaking involving the demolition of the buildings on the south side succeeds, after thirteen centuries the Self-Sprung Temple of Wisdom is likely to fall victim to the accelerating pace of the kaliyuga.

A story of Padma Sambhava at Swayambhunath related in Dudjom Rinpoche's Yid-kyi mun sel relates how the greatest of exorcists transfixed the Lord of the Earth sPrul-lto-nag-po with a phur-ba, and how seven bats and a stone image of gShin-rje-nag-po flew there as protectors. It is said that this image is still worshipped although it has sunk into the ground (Dudjom Rinpoche p.40).

3. SHANTIPUR

'Od-zer Go-cha (Amsuvarman): Santipuri: within the confines of the path which encircles the sacred area of Swayambhu are one hundred temples. In the [temple called Santipuri] Manjughosa's emanation, the Dharmaraja Amsuvarman ('Od-zer Go-cha), met Vajrasattva's emanation, the Acarya Santikar, who had obtained the Body of Immortality. Herein is the mandala drawn in the heart blood of the Eight Great Nagas. Further, here is a temple-place of Mahadeva and Ganapati.

There was once a king of Gauda (in Bihar), an emanation of Vajrasattva called King Pracanda Deva, who decided to make pilgrimage, and leaving his kingdom in the hands of his son, Sakti Deva, having arrived at Swayambhu and taking ordination there, he began the ascetic practices of Vajrasattva. His religious name was Santi Sri (Zhi-ba'i dpal, Santikar). In order to protect the Dharmadhatu Vagisvara Swayambhu Stupa (Chos-bdyings gsung-gi dbang-phyug rang-byung mchod-rten) he covered it with earth and produced the form of a stupa. Also, as an indication of Manjudeva's power, he built a stupa at the place where the Bodhisattva had sat for so long. Thereafter it was called Manjushri's Stupa. Then he built the five shrines of Shantipuri (Akasapuri), Agnipuri, Nagapuri, Vasupuri and Vayupuri. In a year of great misfortune, after no rain had fallen for seven years, the King Gunakamadeva entered Santipur and met the Acarya Santi Sri, begging him to make rain. Santi Sri propitiated the Nagas, summoning them with mantra, and forced them to bring rain. Opposed to this Newar account is the false Tibetan belief that Nagarjuna was the siddha who propitiated the Nagas to make rain. (Chos-kyi Nyi-ma)

The Newar chronicles speak of a King Gunakamadeva who entered the inner sanctum of Santipur to meet Santikar to make rain. Gunakamadeva is said to have been a puppet of Amsuvarman, an interloper who seized power at the beginning of the 7th century and became the greatest of the Nepali Kings of the Licchavi era (Regmi 1969: 161 ff.). The Gunakamadeva of the chronicles is a king of the dvapara-yuga. An historical Gunakamadeva reigned between 987-990, but if Santikar was his contemporary the Acarya could not have established Tantra in the Valley; the 9th century is the latest that Tantra arrived here.

There was another later king, who entered Santipur to make rain. He was Jaya Pratap Malla (reigned 1641-1674), whose inscription upon a stele outside the inner door of Santipur proclaims that he entered in 1658 to bring out into the sunlight the Naga Mandala drawn in the blood of the Eight Naga Kings, together with the Mahamegha-sutra, in order to bring rain. The King caused a map to be drawn describing his peregrinations beneath Santipur. The map shows four levels to the temple. On the ground floor are six empty rooms into which "His Majesty, King of Kings, Lord of Poets, Jaya Pratap Malla Deva entered with puja materials, a fish, black soya beans and cow's milk." There is no indication of a way down to the first subterranean level, and no way out of the room into which he entered on that level except a small niche in the wall. However, in the central room of the first floor he found the Mahasambaratantra, a painting in a copper cylinder, two swords and the Sunyakaru Yantra, and here he discovered the presence of Sri Sri Sri Mahasambara himself. All the other rooms on this level were empty. The King proceeded alone, since "the gubarjus (priests) would not go further as they could not see the way", through a stone door and down into the second subterranean level. In the first room "bats as large as kites or hawks came to kill the light." In the second room "ghosts, flesh-eating spirits and hungry ghosts came to beg. If you are unable to pacify them they clutch at you." In the third room: "If you cannot pacify the snakes by pouring out milk they chase and bind you. Having pacified them you can walk on their bodies." In the central room, "the King met Santikar Acarya, who had become a siddha, sitting in samadhi. He was alive with no flesh on his body. He gave the King instruction, and here the King found the mandala, written in the Naga King's blood, which he took out to make rain". In the next room he sat and meditated and "all things were shown unto him". In the last room was "a hole through which the water of a fathomless lake could be seen [at a third subterranean level]. The waters splash and ripple and the wind blows." The King was below for three hours, and his entourage waited impatiently and in fear for their King who dared to go where no priest dared. Tigers roared and the earth writhed, but finally the King returned and the rains came. The harvest of 1658 was plentiful.[1]

"In Santapuri there is an entrance to three tunnels: a tunnel to Swayambhu Stupa; a tunnel to the Naga Realm; and a tunnel to the realm of obstructive spirits (bgegs). At present there is a six foot square stone covering the entrance. The sixteen volumes of the Prajnaparamitama written upon lapis lazuli paper with ink of gold from the Jumbu River brought from the Naga Realm by Nagarjuna is to be found in the Thang Baidhari of Kathmandu (Thamel Bahal)." Shing-kun dkar-chag A volume of this 'original' Prajnaparamita-sutra is now to be found in the Thamel Bahal (q.v.).

"Nagarjuna was custodian and King Amsuvarman was patron... Santapuri was Nagarjuna's place of meditation... In each of the four cardinal directions of Swayambhu is a treasure trove. These treasure troves were hidden by Nagarjuna for the future restoration of the Stupa... On the eastern flank of the (Vindhya Mountain) is Nagarjuna's meditation cave and the spring he brought forth." (Shing-kun dkar-chag) Nagarjuna ('Conqueror of the Nagas') may have been an epithet of Santikar Acarya, who is not mentioned in the Swayambhu Chronicles; or Santikar Acarya may have been a title of Nagarjuna when he was custodian. The Nagarjuna associated with Santipur may or may not be the same siddha who died in his cave on the hill named after him.

"Santapuri, or Zhi-ba'i grong, is so called because the Vajracarya Santi Deva (God of Peace) called down the god of space (Akasa) and pacified him, and when he remained calm and quiet this place was known as Santapuri. The Santapuri temple was founded during the lifetime of the Acarya Ngag-dbang-grags-pa (Vagisvarakirti), this being the power place where the Acarya attained Rainbow Body and where he remains until this day. The temple has two lower levels, and I have heard that in the deepest of the levels is an image and mandala of Sri Kalacakra... In the environs of Swayambhu many ordinary men have seen what appears to be a stalking tiger who appears out of nowhere and who does no harm to any creature until it vanishes into nothingness; this is generally believed to be Acarya Ngag-dbang-grags-pa revealing his apparitional form... It is said that in one of the Swayambhu Puranas, either the extensive one or the version of middle length, is Acarya Ngag-dbang-grags-pa's biography and other fragments concerning his life. However, this Acarya is numbered amongst the Six Doorkeepers, the Sages of Magadha. Later, at the end of his life, he attained Rainbow Body and still remains here (in Santipur) until this day." Chos-kyi Nyi-ma

It is unfortunate that Chos-kyi Nyi-ma is poorly informed about Santipur, because we are led to doubt his information concerning Vagisvarakirti. Santipur is, of course, Akasapur, (Space-ville). Chos-kyi Nyi-ma is alone in believing that the deity of the secret shrine (the agama-che, usually located on the first floor of the pagoda temple of the viharas) is Kalacakra. This is one of the Valley's principal residences of Cakrasambara, and Santi-deva is not mentioned in any other source as having visited Nepal. Vagisvarakirti's identity is problematic. Pham-mthing-pa's personal name was Vagisvarakirti, and his title was 'Indian', probably indicating that he spent a lot of time on the Plains; he was a master of the Guhyasamaja-tantra and the Cakrasambara-tantra; he lived in the 11th century; his Gurus were Naropa and Savari dBang-phyug (among others). But did he live in Santipur? We agreed with 'Gos Lotsawa that this second Vagisvarakirti was quite distinct from Pham-thing-pa. The Acarya of Santipur is the lineage holder of the Sadangayoga (sbyor drug) of the Guhyasamaja, the six rDzogs-rim practices which lead, not to the Rainbow Body of the rNying-ma-pas, but immortality in a state of suspended animation, all outflows extinct. His predecessor in the lineage was Sakyadhvaja, and his successor was Ratnakirti, also of the 11th century. The Newars believe that Santikar Acarya has remained immured in Santipur since the earliest tantric times. Is it possible that Santikar Acarya was a title of the principal vajracarya of the oldest guthi (circle of initiates) in the valley?

There is no shrine of Mahadeva or Ganapati in the Swayambhu area, but some Hindus will worship the deity of Santipur as Mahadeva.

4. MANJUSRI/SARASWATI HILL

'Jam-dbyangs bzhugs-khri (Manjughosa's Throne): Saraswasti Sthan: at the first, when the Kathmandu Valley was still a lake, Arya Manjusri and his two consorts arriving in the Valley and failing to see [how human beings could worship the Stupa in the middle of the lake], drained the water in three days, and thereafter took their seat upon this spot. [This last line is hopelessly corrupt in Tibetan] The relics of Manjughosa and his two consorts, which remained after their spiritual return to the Five Peaked Mountain in China, are enshrined in a magnificent stupa there. [This line is also a reconstruction].

At the time of the Buddha Visvabhu (the third of the six Buddhas preceding Sakyamuni) Arya Manjusri's emanation, Vajracarya Manjudeva, who was endowed with the five extraordinary powers, came to Nepal from the Five Peaked Mountain in China together with Varada (mChog-sbyin-ma), an emanation of Kesini (sKra-can-ma), and Moksada (gZugs-thar-sbyin-ma), an emanation of Upakeshini (Nye-ba'i Skra-can-ma), in order to see the Swayambhu Dharmadhatu Stupa. Seeing that beings without supernormal powers were unable to worship the stupa in the middle of the lake, he cut a gorge and drained the waters in four days, only a small lake remaining. Then through the Great Master's magical power the lotus, which was the sacred base of the attainment of the Swayambhu Stupa, was transformed into the stupa we know today. At the time of the Buddha Kanakamuni (gSer-thub, the fifth of the seven) the great scholar Dharma Sri Mitra (Chos-dpal bshes-gnyen), lacking knowledge of the Twelve Syllables (?) and on his way from Vikramasila to Manjusri's Five Peaked Mountain for knowledge, found Manjushri himself in the form of Vajracarya Manjudeva and received initiation into the Mandala of Dharmadhatu Vagisvari as the Swayambhu Stupa itself. At the time of the Buddha Kasyapa ('Od-srung, the sixth Buddha), Manjudeva, having accomplished his aim in the form of a vajracarya, took the body of a god and vanished into the sky like a flash of lighting, and returned to the Five Peaked Mountain... Santa Sri built a stupa to mark the spot where he had sat. (Chos-kyi Nyi-ma)

Manjusri Sthan is the western side of the twin peaks of Swayambhu Hill.

5. VIPASWI'S STUPA

mGo-shing prabhat ko cirba (the Gosrnga Parvata Stupa): Where the first of the Seven Buddhas (Vipaswi) had his throne, today a stupa has been erected. In a new monastery in front of this stupa you can see an image of Munindra, the principal image (of five).

Our text locates the Vipaswi Stupa in front of the Dharmacakra Monastery on the northeast side of Manjusri Sthan. The Newars believe that it was Sakyamuni who sat and taught at this spot, which they call Parbatsthan, and that the stupa on the peak of Nagarjuna Hill is Vipaswi's Stupa. This is certainly more rational; but the geography of Li-yul was such that Sakyamuni sat on Gosrnga Parbat and contemplated the Stupa Goma Solagandha from a considerable distance [see Appendix I]. This mis-identification and the mis-naming of Nagarjuna Hill as Ri gLang-ru are both derived from the Gosrnga Vyakarana Sutra.

The Swayambhu Purana tells us that when the Buddha Vipaswi came to the Valley he took his seat upon the hill west of the Lake Nag Hrad, the hill which is now called Jamacho or Nagarjuna, where, from that place he threw a lotus seed into the lake, the seed that would eventually grow into the thousand-petalled lotus upon which the flame of the Swayambhu Dharmadhatu would appear. He foresaw at that time that in the dvapara-yuga the Swayambhu Mandala hill would be called Gosrnga Parvata (Ri glang-ru), the Ox-Horn Mountain.

6. NAGARJUNA HILL

Ri glang-ru lung-bstan (Ox-Horn Prophecy Mountain): Nagarjuna: on top of this mountain, today, a stupa has been built to mark the throne of the Buddha. The Mountain is called Nagarjuna because Nagarjuna's cave-residence is found there.

Again following the Gosrnga-vyakarana-sutra, our text identifies the stupa on Nagarjuna Hill as Sakyamuni's Throne marker, rather than Vipaswi's Stupa. The other sources: Shing-kun dkar-chag; Chos-kyi Nyi-ma; bLa-ma bTsan-po, call the mountain Ri-bo 'Bigs-byed (Vindhya), but also identifies the stupa as Sakyamuni's Throne marker.

"About half a day's journey north of Kathmandu is the Vindhya Mountain." (bLa-ma bTsan-po)

"To the northwest of Swayambhu, on the peak of the Vindhya Mountain is the throne of the teacher Sakyamuni and the thrones of

Sariputra and Maudgalyayana. On the eastern flank of the mountain is Nagarjuna's meditation cave and the spring he brought forth. Very close on the north side are the stupas of Sakyamuni's father, Sodhodana (Sras-gtsang), and his mother, Mayadevi (sGyu-ma Lha-mdzes). On the eastern side of the peak is the place of the Buddha Madhye (Mahe, the Buffalo Buddha). Here is the soil which Halumanyju (Hanuman), the Monkey King, brought from Vulture Peak (?). There are five stupas here. Today there is a Tibetan charnal ground here." (Shing-kun dkar-chag) "In accordance with the prophecy of the Bhagavan (given at Vaisali), at the Lake Gomadeva on the frontier of India, Sariputra and Ananda (Vaisravana in the original Sutra) arising from their thrones, raised their staffs in the air and the lake drained away. Ganapati drained the small amount remaining and then vanished into a rock, and this rock, similar in shape to an elephant, is even now to be seen in the vicinity of the Bungadeo Temple in Patan. (Shing-kun dkar-chag) The Mulasarvastivada Vinaya also reports that the Buddha Sakyamuni's favourite disciple, Ananda, visited the Valley (see Regmi 1969: 279). Maudyalyaya's visit is mentioned in several legends (see infra).

The Vindhya Mountain is called Jamacho in Newari. In front of the Buddha's Throne on the peak is a local cremation ground. In the middle of dense forest beneath the Throne of Sakyamuni is the cave of Nagarjuna in which there are stone images of Nagarjuna and Sakyamuni. Nearby are the tracks of the Mahe Buddha (the Buffalo Buddha). Also nearby is the cave of Acarya Vasubandhu. The two stupas said to be the reliquaries of the father and mother of the Buddha are found on the face of the hill behind (the Balaju) Nilakantha. (Chos-kyi Nyi-ma)

"Nagarjunapad had made a cave on the Jat Matrochcha mountain (Jamacho), where he had placed an image of Akshobhya Buddh, to worship Swayambhu. As the water filled the valley (during the Nagas' attempt to reclaim it from man), it rose up to the navel of this image, whereupon Nagarjun caught the Nag that was playing in the water and making it rise, and confined him in the cave. Whatever water is required in this cave is supplied by this Nag to the present day, and for this reason the Nag is called Jalpurit ('Making Full of Water'). This Nagarjunapad Acharya made an earthen chaitya, and composed or compiled many tantra shastras, and discovered many gods. He died in the cave. The mountain then became known as Nagarjun, and it is considered very sacred. People who are anxious to gain salvation leave orders with their relatives to send their skull-bone (the 'frontal-bone') to this mountain, where it is thrown high in the air, then buried, and a chaitya built over it." (Wright 1972: 96)

There are innumerable caves on the flanks of Nagarjuna Hill. Nagarjuna's Cave still survives high up on the eastern side in a gully. Water flows out of the cave in the monsoon. Images of Nagarjuna and Aksobhya are within. I have not located the Vasubandhu Cave. Nagarjuna's Cave is known to some Tibetans as the cave of Guru Rinpoche (Laksmi Gupha, with its new image of Nagarjuna, is being considered as Nagarjuna's cave). On the north side of the eastern spur, which runs to Balaju, above Raniban Village, is the cave of Bhagavan Buddha. Inside at the back is a seemingly new image of Sakyamuni in bhumisparsa-mudra, a broken image of Bajrabir Mahakala and a stone inscription. Outside is a broken figure in lalita-mudra, probably a form of Tara. There are two empty caves further up the spur. On the north side of the spur is Laksmi Gupha. Inside a steepled chamber within the cave entrance is a relatively new image of Amoghasiddhi or Nagarjuna. During the monsoon of 1980 a large boulder fell from the roof and broke an old image of Vajra Yogini now still visible behind the boulder. Two tunnels barely large enough to allow the passage of a crawling adult lead off from the cavern. One twists and turns for 150' before ending at a figure of the Buddha. The other is equally as long and leads to a chamber with an image of Laksmi. She is visited in times of dire need of wealth. Rumours of caves on Nagarjuna abound. There is reputed to be a cave on this same spur containing a twelve foot high crystal Buddha accessible by rope down a 40' pit and through a narrow tunnel. Further exploration of these caves is needed.

"Nearby the [Nagarjuna Cave] is a cave said by the Tibetans to be the cave of the Buffalo Buddha (Mahe sangs-rgyas shul), which all pilgrims go to see. I asked the Newars the story of the Buffalo Buddha: A long time ago when Acarya Nagarjuna was living in his cave, an idiot buffalo herdsman from Kathmandu became possessed by faith in the Master, and came to him frequently offering curd and milk, etc. Once when he asked Nagarjuna to come to town, the Master refused, saying, 'If you are able to meditate upon perfect reality, sit down here.' So he did as he was told, but obsessed by his work of guarding buffaloes he could think of nothing but buffaloes. 'Visualise yourself as a buffalo.' Instructed the Acarya. So he meditated in what today is called the Cave of the Buffalo Buddha, and after a while he actually became a buffalo. His horns struck the rock above him and the holes which today are known as his horn-prints appeared. Then Nagarjuna told him to contemplate his body in its natural state of total relaxation. Meditating accordingly, his body became as before and his senses became sharp and alert, so he was given initiation and precepts. After he had accomplished the aim of his meditation, it is said that he shot through the roof of the cave and went straight to the Dakini's Paradise (mKha'-spyod). At this power place the horn-prints and the cave with the hole in its roof are clearly visible. (Chos-kyi Nyi-ma)

In style and content this story of the Buffalo Buddha is reminiscent of Abhayadana Sri's Legends of the Eighty Four Mahasiddhas, which recount the mahamudra sadhanas of the Indian siddhas. Many of the siddhas were simple folk, artisans and labourers whose habit patterns (bag-chags) prevented them from meditating on Emptiness (sunyata) and were given creative visualisation (bskyed-rim) of their habitual tasks. Then after the visualisation had become actualised they would be instructed to dissolve their perfect image in the fulfilment process (rdzogs-rim) of identification with their original nature (gnas-lugs or chos-nyid) until they attained mahamudrasiddhi and a transubstantiated body in mKha'-spyod. The thief, Nagabodhi, for instance, was instructed by Nagarjuna to visualise a red horn of avarice protruding from his forehead. When the pain became very severe, he was instructed to meditate upon Emptiness (sunyata) and he quickly gained release.

7. KASYAPA'S STUPA

The reliquary-stupa of the Perfected Buddha Kasyapa lies at the distance of an arrow's flight from Sarasvasti Sthan. A secret entrance to the path to the Naga Realm (Sa-spyod), a naturally formed a stone image of a Naga, Acarya Nagarjuna's reliquary-stupa, and reliquary-stupas of other saints are to be found in the vicinity.

Shing-kun dkar-chag indicates that the Kasyapa whose stupa this is, was the Buddha's disciple, the first Zen Patriarch, rather than his Buddha predecessor: "After the Buddha Sakyamuni's parinirvana, Kasyapa was custodian (of the Swayambhu Stupa). Thereafter, Kasyapa attained parinirvana, and to the west of Swayambhu are the stupas of both Kasyapa and Vasubandhu." (Shing-kun dkar-chag)

Relics of Kasyapa Buddha are said to be enshrined in Boudhnath (Sakya bzang-po), in Katishimbhu (q.v.), in Swayambhunath itself (bLa-ma bTsan-po and Shing-kun dkar-chag), in India (bLa-ma bTsan-po) and in this stupa on Manjusri Hill.

Vasubandhu, the younger brother of Asanga, came to Nepal with a thousand disciples after he had finished his work in India (towards the end of the 5th century). Once when he saw a householder ploughing the fields clothed in religious robes, feeling most disconsolate he recited the dharani of Usnisavijaya backwards three times and passed out of his body. His disciples built his stupa at that spot. (Chos-kyi Nyi-ma)

"In each of the cardinal directions of Swayambhu is a treasure trove hidden by the Master Nagarjuna for the later restoration of the Stupa... [when the axis of the Swayambhu Stupa broke] the King Parthivendra Malla (reigned 1680-1688) received a communication from Ganes and in front of the Kasyapa Stupa he discovered gold treasure." (Shing-kun dkar-chag)

Kasyapa's Stupa is on the north side of Manjusri Hill. Here also is an image of Basuki, or Balasuki Nagaraj, in rough painted stone. Basuki's stone is believed to cover an entrance to the Naga Realm (Sa-spyod?). There are no other stupas in this compound. Vasubandhu's Stupa is identified by some as the large stupa on the saddle between the Swayambhu and Manjusri Hills (Pulan Swayambhu). In the courtyard on top of the Manjusri Hill and further east down to the saddle are many unidentified stupas. The relics of Bhavaviveka (early 6th century?), the dialectician, are believed to be enshrined hereabouts. The Newars, apparently, have no legend concerning the moral remains of Nagarjuna, although he died in his cave on Nagarjuna Hill (Wright 1972: 96).

8. BIDJESWORI

rDo-rje rnal-`byor-ma (Vajra Yogini): Bijeswari Sthan (Vidhyesvari): on the banks of the river (Bisnumati) just below Swayambhu is a group of four Yoginis who spontaneously arose from mKha'-spyod.

The Bahal of Bidjeswori (the Newari form of Vidhyesvari) is in the centre of the extremely powerful and power-bestowing Varahi cremation ground above which vultures hover during the day and in which jackals howl at night. The chief image in the temple of the Bahal is Devi Bhagawani Vidhyadhari Viramante (?) (rJe-btsun bcom-ldan-'das rig-pa-'dzin-ma rnam-par-rtsen-ma), the Divine Pleasure-Giving Knowledge Holder. She is in a flying position, her right leg bent up at the knee behind her, and her left leg pulled up high against her breast with her left arm, which presents a thousand-petalled lotus to her nose. Her right arm is outflung behind her holding a vajra above the sole of her right foot. She holds a khatvanga (trident) in the crook of her arm while it rests on her left shoulder. The image is of vast power in bestowing blessings. She is the heart SAMAYA of Maitripa who carried this symbol of his samadhi in sunyata from India. On her right side is Uddhapada Varahi (Phag-mo gnam-zhabs-ma, Foot-in-the-Sky Varahi); one foot is extended to Brahmaloka (high in the sky), while the other treads furiously down upon a golden Mahesvara. She holds the same emblems as Vidhyesvari. On her left side is the Two Headed Vajra Varahi (rDo-rje Phag-mo Zhal-gnyis-ma); this is the well-known form of Vajra Varahi. These three images are eighteen inches high. To the left of these is Vajra Yogini Naro Khecari (rDo-rje rNal-`byor-ma Na-ro mKha'- spyod-ma) in the form of Cakresvari ('Khor-lo'i dbang-phyug-ma, the Consort of Mahasambara) as a twelve year old virgin. (Chos-kyi Nyi-ma)

Chos-kyi Nyi-ma's above description is precise but for the unaccountable description of Vidhyesvari's emblems as thousand petalled lotus and vajra. In this temple and in the standard iconography she carries a skull-cup (kapala) and curved-bladed knife (kartika, gri-gu); perhaps the Fourth Khams-sprul Rinpoche practised a unique sadhana that employs the symbols he describes. The Varahi cremation ground is none other than Ramadoli [see Karnadip]. The four Dakinis are associated with the Cakrasambara-tantra, which is probably the tantra most commonly practised by the Newars, besides being the principal yi-dam of the bKa'-brgyud-pas. At some time several centuries ago, a separate tantra concerning these four Dakinis must have been revealed. However, this tantra is highly secret and little is known about it outside the caste initiates of Sambara guthis (the covens of tantrikas). Vidhyesvari is also known as Akas Yogini; Uddhapada Varahi is Pham-thing Yogini or Indra Yogini or the Indian Pham-thing's Varahi Khecari' (Chos-kyi Nyi-ma); Naro Khachoma is, of course, Naropa's Dakini. mKha'-spyod is the Dakini's Paradise, and synonymous with 'Dakini' is Khecari, meaning 'Sky-Dancer'.

9. KARNADIP CREMATION GROUND

Dur-khrod Ramadoli: Karabir Maman (Kalavira Smarsana): at the confluence of the Bishnuwati and Bhagwati Rivers is the temple of Bhagawani, who is both demanding and dutiful, and a naturally formed stone image of Mahamaya.

"In the lower west of the town [of Kathmandu] is an image of the rGyal-po sku lgna (pancamurtiraja or pancakayaraja) made from jhekshi and called 'The Obstacle Remover'. Besides it is the Ramadoli Cremation Ground." (Shing-kun dkar-chag)

Contrary to the gNas-yig and Shing-kun dkar-chag, Chos-kyi Nyi-ma locates Ramadoli between Kathmandu and Patan. In his day (18th Century) it was used by Newars, who called it Ramadoli. We must assume an error on his part. He calls Karnadip the Varahi Cremation Ground [see Bidjeswori]. The name Ramadoli is unknown to contemporary Newars, who may recognise the name Karabir Maman but who use the name Karnadip. It is located just south of the confluence of the Bhagawati stream and the Bisnumati, below the Bidjeswori Bahal. Bhagawani or Bhagawati is a powerful form of Durga, known locally as Swobar Bhagawati, and known to the Tibetans as Ekajati. Mahamaya is an epithet of Durga as the Mother Goddess who is the Creatrix, the Universal Illusion, and the Nemesis and Destroyer. The Pancakayaraja made from Jhekshi(?) is most probably a stupa representing the Five Buddhas. Judging from Chos-kyi Nyi-ma's terrific description of the Ramadoli Cremation Ground, that has such an important place in the mythology of the Tibetan's Nepal, it has undergone a radical transformation since the 18th century. Today the Newars cremate their dead on both sides of the river, and for both Buddhist Newars and Tibetans it is the most important cremation ground in Kathmandu; but it is no longer a more fearful place for the sadhaka to meditate then any other cremation ground.

In 1096 Ma-gcig Zha-ma, 'the sole eye of the practitioners on the path of sexual tantra', presented her niece and gold to Dam-pa Sangs-rgyas in return for curing her sexual ailments. Dampa took the niece to Ramadoli where many monks and siddhacaryas were living. (Blue Annals) Obviously Ramadoli was a hive of tantric practice.

In the 15th century, the Mahapandita Vanaratna, the last of the panditas, was cremated at Ramadoli. He had taught many Tibetan disciples many different doctrines, including the Kalacakra-tantra in which he was a realised master. He lived in Santipur Temple on Swayambhu Hill and in the Gopicandra Hermitage (in Patan). (Blue Annals)

10. BURANILAKANTHA

kLu-gan-rkyal (Supine Naga): Narayana Sthan: Buranilakanta (The Old Blue-Throat): the supine image of Visnu at the base of Ox-Horn Mountain (Nagarjuna Hill) was made at a later date by the hand of man, while that on the road to Bagdwar is said to be naturally formed. It is the figure of Visnuraj (Khyab-'jug).

Here is a stone image of Visnu Deva bathing, lying supine in Naga Sesa's bathing pond. (Chos-kyi Nyi-ma)

Lama bTsan-po's description of the Gausainthan Mahadeva fits the Bura Nilakantha Visnu: "Where the stream widens into a pond there is a stone image of a man formed naturally in the rock. It is sky blue in colour and its face is covered with a saffron shawl. It appears to be sleeping on its back [protected by] the hoods of a nine-headed cobra." (bLa-ma bTsan-po)

"The Raja (Jaya Pratap Malla, reigned 1641-1684) had a dream in which he was told by Budha Nilakantha that he or any of his descendants or successors who went to visit Nilkantha would die. Hence, from that time, no Raja ever visits Budha Nilakantha." (Wright 1972: 215)

Wright's chronicles tell how Siva's throat gained a patch (kantha) of blue (nila): "Oh Maharaj, in the Satya Yuga the thirty three crores of gods, devatas, and daityas, churned the ocean, and first of all there came out the Uchchaisrava, which Indra took, saying that it was his luck. After the horse came out Lakshmi, whom Vishnu took. Then came out the Kalakuta poison, and began to destroy the world. The thirty-three crores of devatas began to pray to Mahadeva, who alone was able to destroy the power of the poison. Mahadeva, being easily propitiated, appeared, and asked what they wanted from him. They replied that the Kalakuta poison was destroying the world and themselves, and they sought protection, and implored it with joined hands and tears in their eyes. Mahadeva said that he would instantly destroy its powers; and so saying, he put it into his mouth, but instead of swallowing it, he kept it in his throat, which became blue from the effects of the poison, and hence Mahadeva is named Nila Kantha. Feeling now very hot he went close to the snowy range of mountains, but the cold there was not sufficient to cool him. He then struck his trisul into the mountain, from which sprung three streams of water, and lay himself down and let the water fall on his head. There (in the Gosain Kund Lake, north of the Kathmandu Valley) lies Sadasiva, who takes away the sins of man, and exempts him from rebirth." (Wright 1972: 165)

It is widely believed that the water of both the Budha (Old Budha in Sanskrit, Bura in Newari) Nilakantha and Bala (Young) Nilakantha (at Balaju) springs originate at Gosainkund. Although contemporary legend has it that King Jaya Pratap Malla had the Balaju image made after his dream, like the larger Budha Nilakantha it may well be 7th Century Licchavi. The Balaju image is composite Visnu/Siva: the standard iconography of Jalasayana Visnu (Submarine Visnu) is modified to put Siva's rosary and water-pot in his two upper hands. We have no legend explaining Visnu's association with the Nilakantha story. The Buddhist Newars worship the image as Nilakantha Lokeswara, and a false etymology makes Budha Nilakantha mean Buddha Nilakantha (Pal 1970: 17].

11. THAMEL BAHAL, VIKRAMASILA MAHAVIHARA

The Prajnaparamita in One Hundred Thousand Slokas (Sher-phyin bum) lies in Thamel Bahal. The sacred manuscript text written in gold which Arya Nagarjuna brought from the Naga Realm is to be found in the Bahal Temple.

"The sixteen volume Prajnaparamita written upon paper of lapis lazuli with ink of gold from the `Dzam-bu River and brought by Nagarjuna from the Naga Realm is to be found in the Thang Baidhari of Kathmandu." (Shing-kun dkar-chag)

The temple of Stham Vihara was founded by Jowo Atisa; Pandit Bibhuti Candra lived and taught there; and Savari dbang-phyug taught there. Pan-chen Nags-rin (Vanaratna) also stayed there for some time. (Chos-kyi Nyi-ma)

"Also in Nepal is the Tham Vihara, called the First Vihara or the Upper Vihara. Every evening a light glowed upon a stupa [in this vihara], and when Jowo Atisa saw it he asked everyone what it was but received no information until an old woman told him that it was the red powder of the mandala constructed by the Buddha Kasyapa. Jowo Atisa erected a temple in which to worship the stupa. In front of this stupa is a golden image of Sakyamuni called Lord Abhayadana. Indians call this place the Dharmadhatu Vihara." (Dharmaswamin: folio 6b].

Atisa visited the Valley in 1041, and although he was certainly responsible for establishing the Tham Vihara as a centre of reformed monasticism in a tantric climate, it is certain that there was some foundation there in preceding centuries. Dharmaswamin visited Nepal in the 13th century. For his Tibetan monks, Atisa later evoked this vihara as a model of discipline and study. Throughout the centuries a strong link has been maintained with the Tibetan reformed schools, their pilgrims using the Vihara as a resting place. It seems that the dGe-lugs-pa school had the same relationship with Tham Vihara as the bKa'-grgyud-pas with the Kimdol Vihara. However, of the plethora of names - Thang Baidhari, Stham Vihara, Tham Vihara, Vikramasila Mahavihara, and Thamel Bahal - which have been used to describe this supposedly same Vihara, only the last two are known to the Newars of today, and more research is necessary before we can definitely identify Thamel Bahal with Atisa's vihara.

12. KATISIMBHU

Sa-lhag rdo-lhag mchod-rten: Katishimbu (the Small Swayambhunath): it is said that the stupa of Katishimbu was constructed with the earth and stones remaining from the Swayambhu Stupa, and it is also said that it spontaneously arose through the power of an Indian Siddha. The hair of Sariputra's head is believed to be enshrined therein.

"There is also a stupa [in Kathmandu] said to contain the turban of Arya Sariputra." (bLa-ma bTsan-po)

"In front of the [old] Kathmandu Palace is a gilt copper stupa, the largest of many in Kathmandu, containing the turban of Sariputra and the relics of Kasyapa." (Shing-kun dkar-chag)

Katisimbhu stands in Sighabaha, about half a mile north of the old palace. Its dome is of concrete and its superstructure gilt copper in the same design as Swayambhu Stupa. The meaning of its Tibetan name would presumably indicate that it was built at the same time as the Swayambhu Stupa, i.e. at the time of Santikar Acarya, who was a contemporary of Amsuvarman if we trust the Swayambhu Chronicles (see Santipur) and assume that the Gunakamadeva who is associated with Santipur is the same as the early 7th century king. Thus we could date Swayambhu and Katisimbhu as 7th century constructions. Shing-kun dkar-chag tells us that in the late 17th century Katisimbhu was the largest stupa in Kathmandu. Magnificent Licchavi stone statues attest to the very early glory of Kathisimbhu.

13. ANNAPURNA

Nor-bum (Vase of Wealth): Lachamikalasa (Laksmi Kalasa): in the middle of Asantole Market is a naturally formed stone vase covered in silver in a pagoda temple. Nearby is a temple of Ganapati.

Annapurna is a form of Laksmi, the consort of Visnu, and the goddess of wealth and prosperity. A pot or pitcher (Kalasa) is often found as a representation and symbol of the Devi in her temples. The Annapurna Temple is, perhaps, the most sacred and efficacious of Laksmi's shrines in the Valley.

14. JANA BAHAL - THE WHITE MACCENDRANATH

Jo-bo dzam-gling dkar-mo (po?) (The White Lord of Jambudvipa): Jana Bhal: this image of Avalokitesvara arose from Buddhafields blessed with the power of speech. It is also referred to as Machindharanath (Seto Matsyendranath).

"The White Lord Jamali (Jo-bo `Ja'-ma-li dkar-po) is one of the Five Exalted Brothers ('Phags-pa mched lnga), and the divine essence of these five Brother divinities is Avalokitesvara. The two Brothers who reside in Patan (A-Kham and U-Kham) are red in colour while this one is white, so some believe that he is Manjughosa, which is erroneous." (Chos-kyi Nyi-ma)

"In Kathmandu is the Sandalwood Well (Chandan-gyi khron-chu) out of which the Four Exalted Brothers were born, the White Jamali and Bod-thang mgon-po." Shing-kun dkar-chag

The 14th-15th century Tibetan chronicle rGyal-rabs gsal-ba'i me-long (folio 40bff.), presumably based on the Mani bKa'-bum account, relates to the origin of the Four Exalted Brothers: The Emperor Srong-btsan sGam-po (7th century) sent a priest to Nepal to bring back an image of Avalokitesvara. In a forest on the edge of the Valley the priest discovered a sandalwood tree that was being nurtured with the milk of a buffalo. This magical tree commanded the priest to cut it down, and then four images appeared out of it: 'Phags-pa Wa-ti, 'Phags-pa U-Gang, 'Phags-pa Jamali, and 'Kasyapani' Buddha (Kharsapana Lokesvara?). The priest took the first to Mang-yul (Kyirong), the second to Yam-bu (Kathmandu, though U-Gang is in Patan), the third to the border (Kojarnath?), and the fourth to Lhasa.

In the traditional Tibetan accounts the Four Exalted Brothers are associated with the Emperor Srong-btsan sGam-po who is credited with bringing the cult of Avalokitesvara to Tibet, but there appear to be varying opinions as to the identification of the fourth Brother. The three in which all sources can be made to agree are 'Phags-pa U-Gang in Patan, 'Phags-pa Wa-ti in Kyirong and the Lhasa Lokesvara in the Potala. The fourth Brother, 'Phags-pa Jamali, is located both in Kojarnath near Taklakot, northeast of Almora in Tibet (see Wylie 1970: 20), and in Kathmandu in Jana Bahal. Chos-kyi Nyi-ma counts five Brothers by adding A-Gang (q.v.) in Patan. The Lama of Kojarnath avers that the fourth Brother is the Kathmandu Jamali (Wylie 1970: 20). The local Newari legends associated King Gunakamadeva with the origins of the Jamali cult, and one king of that name was a contemporary of King Amsuvarman and the Emperor Srong-btsan sGam-po. Furthermore, the Newari legends mention that Jamali was stolen by 'a Magala King from the west'. The Western Mallas ruled over Kojarnath from the 10th to the 13th centuries and it is possible that Jamali was taken hostage by a Malla King and later reclaimed by the Valley people - the vamsavalis mention other cases of images being stolen by invading Tibetans. Jamali appears again in Kathmandu in Yaksa Malla's time (1428-1480), when he was found in a well (or in a field) in Jamal, which is the area south of the present royal place. It was probably in Yaksa Malla's time that Jamali was taken from its Jamal location and placed in its present position in Jana Bahal (Kanaka Caitya Mahavihara) near Indra Chowk. (See Locke 1980: 147ff.)

The plastered image in the freestanding Jana Bahal Temple is of Padmapani Lokesvara, white in colour, about 4' high. He wears the Bodhisattva crown and ornaments, and the figure of Amitabha is painted in the centre of his jata. On his right and left are the White and Green Taras. The kwapadeo (principal deity of the Bahal) is Aksobhya. The Newars call Jamali 'Jama Deo' or 'Karunamaya Lokeswar'. To the Hindus this deity is the patron saint of the Valley, Seto Matshendranath. He is given suitable honour by the entire town in Kathmandu's greatest khat festival. An interesting feature of the Jana Bahal temple is the glass-framed paintings of Avalokitesvara's 108 forms hung below the first floor of the pagoda temple. (See Locke 1980)

15. THE ITUM BAHAL TALKING TARA

sGrol-dkar (White Tara): Sheto Tara: she is located in Itum Bahal. She is said to have flown there from Tibet and is called the Talking Tara.

This White Tara is found in a side courtyard (nani bahal) of the vast Itum Bahal, which is north of the old palace. Itum Bahal is one of

Kathmandu's oldest bahals. It is associated with the cannibal demon Guru Mapa and a certain Kescandra who traded with him (see Wright 1972: 169). The name Mahasantasvetadharmacakratara is inscribed on the temple wall.

16. THE MAKHANTOLE STONE ARROW

Sang-rgyas rdo-mda' (The Buddha's Stone Arrow): rMa-khan tol ko sa trag ko dhung ga (the stone satrag (?) of Makhantol).

In the middle of the town of Kathmandu there is a stone arrow thrown from the top of the Vindhya Mountain by the Bhagavan, Sariputra and Maudgalyayana that has remained there until this day. (Shing-kun dkar-chag)

According to the Newar tradition, Manjusri shot three arrows from the peak of Nagarjuna to determine the depth of the lake that filled the Valley. One landed in Chabahil where it wounded a Naga, who after Manjusri's successful ministrations became Ganapati's vehicle at Chabahil Ganesthan, healing sick supplicants; one landed in Asantole; the third landed in Makhantole where it is visible in a shallow hole on the western side of the road beside the lion guarding the entrance to the square from the Indra Chowk side. Another local Newar informant believed that the arrow had been shot by a Buddha in Lhasa.

17. KALA BHAIRAB

mGon-po phyag-drug-pa (Six-Armed Mahakali): Kala Bhairab: this is located in front of Hanuman Doka. Behind this image within a lattice screen of red wood which is part of the palace wall, [and which is built upon] a long straight stone, is a likeness of Mahakala's face fashioned by the hand of the Lord Karmapa.

Bhairab, as in this Hanuman Doka image, holds the skull bowl (kapala) in the right hand while his left hand shows the uyakhyana-mudra (holding ring finger to thumb). Mahakala holds the skull bowl in his left hand and the knife-lid (karpatra) in his right. Nepalis come to Bhairab to swear oaths, for if a lie is told in his presence the victim will die vomiting blood. At the Dasain festival hundreds of buffaloes are sacrificed to Kala Bhairab. 'The head of Mahakali' is known to Nepalis as Bhairab's head, and there is no known connection with the Karmapa. Pratap Malla (reigned 1641-1674), Kathmandu's great beautifier, the hero of Santipur, claims in one of his numerous inscriptions to have built Kala Bhairab. However, Mahakala is the principal protector of the Karmapas.

18. THE GREAT BELL

Dril-chen: thulo ghanti: near the great bell is a large drum.

Located on the west side of the old palace is the great bell, and nearby in a covered, three-walled shed is a pair of large kettle drums.

19. KUMARI'S PALACE

mKha'-`gro-ma'i pho-brang (the Dakini's Palace): Kumari Bhal: to the south of the [old] palace resides a virgin who is a living Dakini. Go there rendering prostration and offering and solicit the omens of her speech.

The Kumari is worshipped as a living emanation of Taleju Bhawani, a form of Durga and the patron goddess of the Valley's kings. Her palace in Basantapur was built by Jaya Prakas Malla, the last of the Malla kings, who initiated the royal worship of the Virgin. The Gorkhali Shaha kings continued her worship, and this virgin, pre-pubescent girl may be considered the only human being superior in status to the king. After she bleeds in any way she is replaced. She then marries into the Sakya caste as any other Sakya maiden. She is known as the Raj Kumari, the Royal Virgin. Insofar as Hindus identify Tara as an aspect of Durga as in the dasamahavidhya, the Kumari is sometimes referred to as Tara. The Bhaktapur Taleju is sometimes referred to as Tara. The Bhaktapur Taleju is sometimes confused with Tara. Buddhists worship Kumari as Vajra Yogini, whose image is found in the inner temple of Kumari Bahal. As the sakti of the virgin youth Kumari, the son of Siva, also known as Skandha and Karttikeya, Kumari is identified with the matrka Kumari. (See Allen 1975)

20. MARU SATTAL

Mahaguru Sang-rgyas gnyis-pa'i bzhugs-khri (the Throne of the second Buddha, the Mahaguru Padmasambhava, Guru Padma): Maru satal ko asan (the Maru Sattal Seat of Meditation): this temple was constructed out of a single tree trunk. Inside is an amazing bean-stalk 27 pillar, an image in the likeness of Guru Gorakhnath, and four images of Ganapati.

In the centre of the ground floor of this large pagoda temple cum rest-house is the image of Gorakhnath with long hair, large ear-rings, his left arm resting upon a stick, and sitting in padmasan – the archetypal kanphata yogin. In the corners of the inner forum are the four Ganapatis - Surya Vinakaya,

Karya Vinayaka, Jal Vinayaka and Asoka Vinayaka. Perhaps the 'bean-stalk pillar' 'refers to the several thin 20' high pillars that support the upper floors of the pavilion; otherwise, it must refer to something that has vanished in the last 150 years. The present structure is a mandapa or sattal called Kasthamandapa because, according to the Newar legend, it was constructed from a single tree trunk; the year was 1143, before the Malla ascendency, and the mainspring in its construction was a Saiva siddha called Lopipada. It is among the oldest structures in the country and the largest of its type. Mandapa is best translated as 'pavilion' since its floors are open and raised on pillars, and it functions as a rest-house, temple and village hall. A sattal has virtually the same functions, but it is usually partly enclosed and without a shrine. This madnapa-sattal has three floors, the ground floor being used as a community-meeting place with the shrine of Gorakhnath in the centre, and the second and third floors were employed by the nath akara as living space for itinerant yogins until the government evicted them in 1966 when the mandapa was fully restored for the umpteenth time. Literary evidence exists that the site was occupied by a religious foundation in the 11th century, during the time of Gorakhnath, and if indeed this is the E Vihara of the Tibetans' tradition a Buddhist vihara occupied the site at least as long as the 8th century. This manapa was given to the nath akara in the 14th century and has remained in its hands ever since. (See Slussor 1974)

"The E Vihara Temple, known as the Kathmandu Valley E Vihara (Bal-yul E-yi gtsug-lag-khang), is the place referred to in the bKa'-thang gter-mas where the Great Master Padmasambhava taught the Newari girl, Kusali, stories about hell." (Chos-kyi Nyi-ma)[2]

"The Great Saint of Uddiyana spent three lunar months in Nepal./ After granting great benefactions to the Nepali Vasudhara and many others in Nepal,/ He hid a treasure in the monastery of E Kara. Then in the grotto of Yanglesho (q.v.), in that of the Asura (q.v.) and other grottos,/ In the monastery of Shanku [q.v.] and other Nepali monasteries,/ At the crag called Mighty Soil and other places round about, he hid 1000 other treasures." (Urgyan gLing-pa: 365) "gTsug-la dPal-dge will reveal the treasure of the E Vihara." (Urgyan gLing-pa: 621)

Ye-shes mTsho-rgyal, Guru Padma's Consort, visited Kathmandu Valley in the 8th century soon after Guru Padma had passed through on his way to Tibet, and had encountered one Vasudhara. She was accompanied by her recently purchased partner in yoga called Sa-le, an Indian slave owned by a Bhaktapur household. She met Vasudhara in the E Vihara. (sTag-sham Nus-ldan rDo-rje)

The rdzogs-pa anuyoga lineage began with King Dza, who received instructions from Vajrapani (gSang-ba'i bdag-pa) himself, and it descended through the Indian siddhas: Indrabodhi, Kukuraja, dGa'-rab rDo-rje, Prabahasti, Sakyamitra, Dhanaraksita, Humkara and bDe-ba gSal-mdzad. The latter had four disciples of whom two were gTsug-la dPal-dge and Vasudhara. Both of these taught Sangs-rgyas Ye-shes of gNubs who was the progenitor of the Tibetan lineage. The gter-ston of E Vihara, gTsug-tag dPal-dge, must have been a later incarnation of the anuyoga lineage holder who himself studied in Nepal and knew the E Vihara, he followed soon after the first gter-ston Sangs-rgyas bLa-ma, who lived in the 11th century. Vasudhara is referred to as 'King of Nepal'; but he was more likely to have been a renunciate feudatory prince, or simply a Ksatriya. His Gurus were Guru Padma, Dhanaraksita and Che-btsan-skyes of Gilgit (Brusa). Vasudhara must have been an outstanding scholar-yogin of his time (8th century), and the E Vihara an important centre of vajrayana when the new cult of tantra was still the prerogative of visiting Indian siddhas and a few Nepali yogins. (See Dudjom Rinpoche 1967: 56a ff.)

This Vasundhara may well be the same Newar who visited Tibet during Khri-srong lDe-btsan's reign, at the same time as Vimalamitra, Buddhagupta, Kamalasila, et al, to assist in the work of translation and in the instruction of the Tibetan neophytes. However, no Nepali is counted amongst the 25 panditas invited to Tibet from the Indian sub-continent by Khri-srong lDe-btsan.

Gorakhnath is known in Tibet from the 'Legends of the Eighty Four Mahasiddhas (Grub-thob brgyad-bcu tsa bzhi'i lo-rgyus)' – a translation into Tibetan of the Pandit Abhayadana Sri's stories of the siddhas. Gorakhnath was a cow-herd who was called upon by the siddha Jalandhara to tend an unfortunate prince who had had his legs cut off and who had been left to die in the jungle. Gorakhnath performed this task with devotion and assiduity for 12 years, and this practice of selfless service being the equivalent of preliminary purificatory yogic sadhana, after he had received instruction from his Guru Jalandhara he soon attained mundane siddhi. However, he never attained mahamudra-siddhi, the acme of Buddhahood attained by eighty-two of the eighty-four mahasiddhas. He achieved immortality, and was exhorted to spend his days in the conversion of sentient beings, with the proviso that he should not teach those who were not prepared or karmically matured. Thus this legend agrees with the common belief amongst Indians that Gorakhnath is still alive, like other great siddhas who achieved immortality during the flowering of tantra between the 9th and 12th centuries, and that he is still teaching in the Himalayas to those fortunate beings whose karma is ripe and have eyes to see him.

21. TONDIKHEL BAJRABIR MAHAKALI

Bod-thang mgon-po: Mahakala: in Tongtikhel is a particularly sacred, naturally formed stone image of Mahakala.

"Some say that the Bod-thang-mgon-po is naturally formed. Others believe that he was constructed by the very hands of the Great Master Nagarjuna, that Nagarjuna made 108 images of Mahakala and that among the protectors he appointed to protect the great power places such as Vajrasana (Bodh Gaya), this was the one he appointed to protect the Swayambhu Stupa. However he was formed, this amazing image possessed of superior powers of conferring grace is a climactic attainment. This protector of the Innate (sahaja), this Root Protector, is made of black stone. He has one face and two hands holding a skull-cup (kapala) of blood and a curved-bladed knife (kartika) at his heart. He carries a trident (katvanga) on his shoulder, corpse. A long time ago, an invading army of Muslims came to this valley they were unable to complete his destruction, and in this land of Nepal the Muslim doctrines never made any inroads. However, there was slight damage done to the image at that time, to some parts of the corpse, to Mahakala's body and to the tip of his nose... This image previously sat on the top of the Phullado Hill (Pulchowk) close to Patan, and because it came flying through the sky [to this spot] it became known as 'The Arrival in Tibetan Fields' (Bod-thang du phebs). Concerning the name Bod-thang (Tibetan Fields), the site of the temple was the spot to which the King Amsuvarman sent his daughter, Bhrkuti (Bal-mo bza' khri-btsun); the Tibetan messengers, some ministers of the Dharmaraj Srong-btsan sGam-po and others, waited for her there; thus 'Tibetan Fields'." (Chos-kyi Nyi-ma)

The Red Annals, a 14th century historical work based on highly regarded Chinese originated sources, reports that Amsuvarman (Od-gser Go-cha) gave Srong-btsan sGam-po. his daughter Bhrkuti in marriage and that the image of the Buddha called Jo-bo Mi-skyod rDo-rje and a sandalwood statue were given as dowry. The Nepali image of Jo-bo was housed in the so-called Lhasa Cathedral (sDeb-ther-dmar-po f.16b).

The detailed account of the manner in which Bhrkuti was procured from Amsuvarman is found in the 12th chapter of the important history rGyal-rabs gsal-ba'i me-long (15th century) is based on the legendary account of the gter-ma Mani bka'-bum (or an older source common to both). The emperor sent his minister mGar-ba to Nepal with a large force of cavalry (rTa-dmang = Tamang). He finds Amsuvarman in Bhaktapur (Kho-khom). Having presented five square gold coins and a suit of armour inlaid with turquoise, the minister makes his request. Amsuvarma is at first scornful but upon the receipt of correct answers to his three questions, which the Emperor had anticipated, regarding the moral law, temples and mineral wealth of Tibet, and threatened by Tibetan military invasion, Amsurvarman accedes to mGar-ba's request. Bhrkuti takes an image of Mi-skyod rDo-rje (Kasyapa Buddha), a dharmacakra, a turquoise begging bowl and a sandalwood image of Tara to Tibet as a dowry. In Lhasa she is responsible for the construction of the Potala palace and the Ra-sa `phrul-snang temple on the site of a drained lake. Many other temples in Tibet are attributed to her. It is noteworthy that Nepali craftsmen cast and carved images in Lhasa at this time, and that the Nepali Sila Manju was among the scholars that Emperor invited to Tibet.

Regarding the Tibetan legends of Amsuvarman's daughter, Bhrkuti, marrying King Srong-btsan sGam-po of Tibet, Nepali and some western historians are incredulous. Some difficulties of chronology support their scepticism; but the Mani bka'-bum was almost certainly based on a much earlier, authoritative text. If the early date for Srong-btsan's birth, 569, is rejected, and we assume that he was born in the now generally accepted year 617, Bhrkuti must have been born the daughter of Amsuvarman's old age between 617 and the year of his death, 620-621, to be a suitable 16 year old bride for the Tibetan king. This is consistent with the 634-635 date (see rGyal rabs gsal-ba'i me'-long f.46b) given as the time of Bhrkuti's arrival in Tibet (she founded the Potala palace in 635), and the texts' unanimous assertion that she married the king before her rival, the Chinese princess Wencheng Kongjo, arrived in 642. It has been suggested that Bhrkuti was the sister of Narendradeva, the great Licchavi king of Nepal (see Macdonald et al 1979: 19, and also Regmi 1969: 186). Narendradeva was placed on the throne by Srong-btsan's invading Tibetan forces who in 642 defeated and killed Jisnugupta (see Choephel 1978: 65), an Indian Avir King who had conquered the country in the wake of Amsuvarman's death. If Bhrkuti had come from

Narendradeva, obviously she would not have been Amsuvarman's daughter and she could not have arrived in 634-635 or before the Chinese princess. However, it would have been highly expedient, politically, for Narendradeva to give a wife to Srong-btsan, the scourge of Central Asia. The only difficulty of accepting that Bhrkuti was Amsuvarman's daughter and that she arrived in Tibet in 634-635 is that Amsuvarman was not alive to negotiate the marriage settlement. A son of Amsuvarman ruled for a time during the troubled and undocumented period after his father's death, and he may provide the answer. But until more evidence is available there is no good reason to reject the evidence of so many Tibetan legends and deny Bhrkuti's Tibetan marriage.

According to an inscription found on Swayambhu Hill set up to commemorate the restoration of the Stupa, in the year 1349 Nepal was invaded by an army of iconoclastic Muslims led by the Sultan Shams Ud-din of Bengal. On its short tour of spoilage, rape and plunder, this army burnt the vihara town of Patan, the principal town of the Valley, broke the Pasupati lingam into four pieces and seriously damaged Swayambhunath.

22. BAGDWAR

Sangs-rgyas 'khor-ba-'jig-gi gnas (The Power Place of the Buddha Krakucchanda): Bagduwar: at this place the Buddha brought forth water from a rock with his index finger. It is called [Bagduwar because the rock from which the water flows] is shaped like a bhaga (vagina).

This entry refers to a story from the Swayambhu Purana: in the tretayuga, the fourth Buddha, Krakucchanda, appeared on earth and came to Nepal to pay homage to Guhjeswori, Swayambhu Dharmadhatu and Manjusri's Throne. He then went to Sankha Parvata (Sivapuri) to preach the Aryasatya, the sublime truth, and many people came to hear him, all of them requesting to be ordained and initiated. Since there was no water on Sankha Parvata, Krakucchanda created a spring through the power of his voice, and this stream was called the Bagmati (Vak-mati = stream of word or mantra). Its water has the power to cure leprosy and to wash away sin. Krakucchanda gave Bagmati the freedom to flow where she would, and ordained that wherever another stream entered hers there should be a sacred bathing place and a spot where the Nagas would be propitiated (a tirtha). Then wherever the hair of Krakucchanda's disciples fell a spring sprung forth, springs which combined to form the Kesavati (the Bisnumati), the second major river of the Valley.

Bagdwar is located on the north side of Sivapuri Hill. The Bagmati flows east to break through the ridge bounding the Valley on the north side at Sundarijal. The power places where ritual bathing is regularly performed along its course are Gokarna, Guhjeswori, Gauri Ghat, Pasupati, Sankhamul, the confluence of Bagmati and Binsumati, and at Chobar. The twelve tirthas of the twelve Nagarajas are also located at confluences along the Bagmati and Bisnumati; but the Nagas are sadly neglected these days. Besides the etymology of Bal-po gnas-yig and that of the Swayambhu Purana, there is a third definition of Bagdwar: because the water flows out through a gargoyle shaped like a tiger's mouth, Bagdwar means 'Tiger Gate'. Thus we have a triad of definitions: tantric, mahayanic and animistic.

23. THE GOLDEN TEMPLE OF PATAN

Ye-rang shakya-thub-pa (Patan Sakyamuni): Shakyamuni Buddha: there is a wonderful temple in the Bahal of Shakyamuni Buddha.

The Vihara of Sakyamuni Buddha is known as Hiranyavarna Mahavihara (The Golden Temple) in Sanskrit and Kwabahal in Newari. The Kwapa-deo (principal image) is Sakyamuni Buddha arrayed in Sambhogakaya ornaments.

24. MAHABOUDHA OF PATAN

Ye-rang sangs-rgyas stong sku (the Thousand Buddhas of Patan): Mahabuddha: this is an attractive stupa made of stone and mud.

Stupa, here refers to the Indian style of temple which has a tower or stupa (gandola) above the shrine. The Mahaboudha temple in Oku Bahal is a replica of Vajrasana (bLa-ma bTsan-po). It was built in the 17th century (1601) by a certain Abhayaraja. Contemporary descendants of Abhayaraja belong to the Sakya caste.

"Concerning the Vajrasan gandola structure (of Mahaboudha), an ancestor of the contemporary (i.e. 18th century) Pandit Ramanda, a Brahmin, in order to increase his power and wealth, actually went to the Holy Land of Vajrasan (Bodh Gaya), and after he returned from his pilgrimage he built a replica of the Vajrasan gandola (dri gtsang khang). The blessed stone image of Buddha brought from Vajrasan itself resides here in the mode of enlightenment (byang-chub-sems-po)." (Chos-kyi Nyi-ma)

25. MINANATH AND MACCHENDRANATH OF PATAN

Ye-rang A-khang U-khang: Minanath and Machindharanath: there is an amazing story of Nrtyanath's (Gar-gyi dbang-phyug's) emanation (of Bungha Deo).

"In Nepal is the sublime Bu-kham temple in which is an image of Avalokitesvara, naturally formed in sandalwood, as a five year old boy, red in colour. This sublime Bu-kham is well known in India while in Tibet the Sublime Swayambhunath is extolled." (Dharmaswamin: folio 6a)

U-khang, Bhu-kham or 'Bu-kham is known as Bunga Deo or Karunamaya to the Newars; and also as Lokeswara and Karujuju (bLa-ma bTsan-po). To the Nepali Hindus he is known as Rato Matsyendranath, the Guru of Gorakhnath and the patron siddha of the Valley. His original residence is Bungamati (hence Bungadeo), but for six months of the year he lives in Tabahal in Patan. His image is of roughly hewn wood, three feet high, with detachable arms, a standing figure covered with clay, and painted red annually. His ratha festival is one of the most significant jatras of the year. (See Locke 1980) Both A-kham and Bu-kham belong to the family of the Five Exalted Brothers (Jo-bo mched lnga), both being forms of Avalokitesvara (Chos-kyi Nyi-ma) [see Jana Bahal]. The Mani bka'-bum dates the Four Exacted Brothers as 7th century images.

"Some Tibetan chronicles, based on Newari oral legend, say that Bu-kham is actually 'Bu-kham ('bu - insect) since this Jowo was born from light emanating from the heart of A-kham in the form of an insect." (Chos-kyi Nyi-ma) This legend probably indicates the greater antiquity of the A-kham cult, a supposition supported by Newari legend and the fact that Minanath is Macchendranath's Guru. A-kham is Padma Nrtyanath, who takes central place in the torana above the main door of the temple, and he is Jatadhari Lokesvara indicating Avalokitesvara as a siddha. His image is a small red Padmapani Lokesvara, standing with his right hand in varada-mudra and his left hand holding a white lotus (see Locke 1980).

Minanath, like Gorakhnath, is known to the Tibetans from Abhayadana Sri's Legends of the Eighty Four Mahasiddhas. Minanath was a Bengali fisherman who hooked a fish at the end of his line that was too heavy to handle. The fish pulled him into the ocean and swallowed him, and he lived in the fish's belly for twelve years. One day the fish swam close to mahadeva who had settled himself at the bottom of the ocean in order to teach Uma, his Consort, a secret dharma. Minanath overheard the instruction. Soon after the fish was caught and the sadhaka liberated from the belly, Mina found that he had gained siddhi, but like Gorakhnath the ultimate realisation of mahamudra escaped him.

There is a Nepali cycle of legends that treats the relationship between the three great Gurus of the Valley (Mina, Goraksa or Gorkhnath, and Macchendranath), which is a lore unto itself. In the Indian tradition of the siddhas, Macchendranath or Matsyendranath can be identified with either Luipa, the fish-gut eater, or Minanath. Unfortunately we do not have any authoritative biographical data that could form a framework for a coherent story based on the legends provided by the different Indian, Tibetan and Nepali cultural traditions.

26. LAKE TAUDAH

mTsho ral-gri (Knife Lake): Ta'uda: when the Kathmandu Valley was drained, the water remaining settled in this lake. Pal-rgyal (King Pala?) set out for the Naga realm from here.

Lake Taudha is the residence of the Nagaraj Karkotaka. (Chos-kyi Nyi-ma)

The ancient name of this lake was Madhara (Kun-'dzin); in Chos-kyi Nyi-ma's time the Newars called it Dhanadaha (Gift-Lake) and the Tibetans Ral-gri (Knife-Lake); today it is called Taudah (Great Lake). It is one mile south of the Chobar gorge on a broad terrace above the river level. It is strange that earthquakes have not emptied it. The local belief is that the wealth of Karkotaka and his Nagas lie concealed within the lake, which is of profound depth. It is said that the Rana overlords of the last century attempted to drain this lake to gain its treasure and were foiled only by its vast depth.

The story of Karkotaka and the Baid (Veda = doctor) describes the Nagaraj's palace. Karkotaka in the guise of a Brahmin sought help from a Baid to heal his wife's eye affliction. The Baid agreed to lend his assistance and accompanied the Naga to Taudah. The pond was so deep, and the water so black, that it was frightful to look at. It was shaded by trees, large fish played in it, and it was covered with watefowl. The Nag told the Baid to shut his eyes, and in a moment he jumped with him into the water and they arrived at the durbar of Nag-raj in Patalpuri. The walls of the palace were of gold, the windows of diamond, the rafters and beams of sapphires, the pillars of topaz adorned with rubies. The darkness of the subterranean palace was dispelled by the light of large jewels in the heads of the Nagas. They entered the palace, and saw the Nagini, sitting on a throne studded with jewels of several sorts, shaded by three umbrellas of white diamonds, one above the other, and surrounded by beautiful Naginis. Karkotak, assuming his proper form, took the Baid by the hand, and gave him a seat near the throne." The Baid cured the Nagaraja's wife's eye disease and was suitably rewarded, but before he left the palace he promised that his descendants would be equally good eye doctors. (Wright 1972: 179).

27. YANGLESHO

Yang-le-shod: Seg Narayana Sthan: on the road to Pharping is the great power place where the Second Buddha Mahaguru subdued gods, spirits and demons.

"Yanglesho in the Kathmandu Valley is the power place of the Great Master Padma `Byung-gnas (Padma Sambhava), and the name of this place is blown on the wind to all, to the wise and the ignorant in the valley of Tibet, the Land of Snow Mountains. And since the Buddhists of Nepal accept this as the power place of the Uddiyana vajracarya Padmakara, they are in agreement with the Tibetans. The Hindus believe that this is the residence of Sesa Narayana, both the Naga 'Remainder' (kLu lhag-ma-can) and Visnu. However, the Gubarjus have only this legendary indication of the place which relates to the Buddhist ethos: When the Great Master Padma 'Byung-gnas himself was sitting at this place in samadhi, through the Naga's magical devices a plethora of venomous snakes appeared, hanging down from above; disturbed by this temptation, the Guru, with a fixed gaze, struck the Naga on the crown of his head with a vajrakila (rdo-rje phur-ba) and turned the menacing serpents into stone. Even today on the crag [overhanging the temple] many serpentine shapes are to be seen struggling downwards. From the trace of the kila on the crown of the head of the central snake, water emerges at certain auspicious moments. The Hindus have many legends, supposedly edifying, which I have listened to with reservations in my mind; amongst the stories of Parasuram, dGar-sta(?) Ramana (=Vamana?) one (or two?) of the ten incarnations of Visnu, the emergence of water from the trace of the kila is said to be the emergence (of milk?) from the cow, which gives milk eternally, and so on... The Great Master Padma 'Byung-gnas, having previously practised various ascetic yogas in cremation grounds, took to wandering, and at that time he received initiation from Vajra Varahi, attaining the Knowledge Holder of Spiritual Maturity (rnam-par-smin-pa'i rig-'dzin) and gaining victory over the 'devil of corporeality'. At the cave of Maratika (Heileshe, east of Okoldunga and south of Mt. Everest) he attained the Knowledge Holder of Immortality (tshe-la dbang-ba'i rig-'dzin), gaining victory over the devil 'Lord of Death'. At Yanglesho he attained the Mahamudra Knowledge Holder (phyag-chen rig-'dzin), gaining victory over the 'devil of emotivity'. At Vajrasan (Bodha Gaya) he attained the Knowledge Holder of Spontaneity (lhun-gyi-grub-pa'i rig-'dzin), gaining victory over the 'godling devil'. Amongst these four Knowledge Holder attainments the mastery of Mahamudra is the ultimate, unsurpassable, supreme attainment, and since the Guru achieved it in Yanglesho, this place is of equal significance to Vajrasan [where Sakyamuni attained enlightenment] for the Guhyamantra rNying-ma-pa school. (Chos-kyi Nyi-ma)

In Guru Padma's biographical bKa'-thangs it is not made clear exactly how he divided his practice between the cave at Yanglesho and the Asura Cave; but it my be inferred that his mahamudra practice is associated with the former, and the practice of Yang-dag and Phur-ba with the latter. This is an adaptation of the 5th chapter of the bKa'-thang zangs-gling-ma, a revealed text (gter-ma) of Nyang-ral Nyi-ma `Od-zer (1124-1192 A.D.), which describes Guru Padma's accomplishment of the Mahamudra Knowledge Holder, by means of Yang-dag and Phur-ba combined, at Yanglesho: Then the Guru thought to himself, 'Although I have attained the Knowledge Holder of Immortality, there is no advantage unless I attain the Mahamudra Knowledge Holder.' So he came to the meditation cave at Yanglesho between India and the Kathmandu Valley, to the Tree of Generosity that never withers in winter. Here he captivated a highly qualified yogini, called Sakya Devi (Sakya bDe-mo), and began his practice with the Mandala of Glorious Yang-dag's Nine Lamps. Obstacles immediately arose. The Nagas, Raksasas and Sky-Demons conspired to cause a three year drought and famine in Nepal, Tibet and Indian, and plague struck both men and cattle. The appearance of Death provoked Guru Padma to the realisation that he must destroy the power of those demons if he was to attain mahamudra, and giving an ounce of gold dust to his Nepali disciples Jila Jisad and Kun-la ku-bzhi, he sent a plea to his pandita Gurus in India to send the means to achieve the subjection of the obstructing spirits. He was instructed to apply to Prabhahasti, which he did, and he received the text of the Phur-ba

Vitotama, which two men could barely carry. Immediately upon the appearance of the text in Yanglesho, the ocean threw up gifts, the earth was suddenly fertile and clouds gathered in the sky. Rain fell upon the parched soil and simultaneously shoots, levels, buds and fruit matured. By eating this fruit both men and cattle were cured of disease and the Kingdom was filled with happiness and laughter. At this time, Guru Padma had a vision of the retinues of both Yang-dag and Phur-ba. Attaining identity with Yang-dag he gained great siddhi, but obstacles arose too; then upon rDo-rje Phur-ba's entourage's manifestation all obstacles disappeared. Then practising their combined rites (Yang-dag phur-ba 'brel-ba) he attained Supreme mahamudra-siddhi. Through that night, at evening, at midnight and before dawn, various spirits came to him offering their life-essence, and he bound them all to pledges to serve as rDo-rje Phur-ba's Logos Protectors (bKa'-srung). The Four bSe-mo Sisters, the Four Sho-na-ma Sisters, the Four Remati Sisters and the families of the Four Bse-yi skyes-bu, the Four Iron Beings (lCags-kyi skyes-bu), and the Four Conch beings (Dung gi skyes bu) wer all bound in this way. Thus Guru Padma overwhelmed the arrogant spirits of the Mandala of Divine Form: he brought all sound and vibration of the Mandala of Mantra under his control; and every mental construct and thought, and all of the five poisons, were rendered void as they arose into the mandala of the True Nature of Mind, into the reality of indeterminate, non-conceptual purity. In the plenum of Innate purity he entered the Unchangeable Mind of Mahamudra."

Another account tells of how Ting-lo-sman of the north, sTag-sman-zor-bar-gdong and Byang-phug bsTan-ma-bcu-gnyis sent a storm down upon Guru Rinpoche while he was staying at Yanglesho, paralysing his entourage with cold. The Guru pointed his fingers in mudra of threat and a firestorm emanating from his fingers raged around the snow and shale mountains where the gods dwelt. Then they all came to him offering him their lives. [Dudjom Rinpoche, Yid-kyi mun sel: 44a)

If you look through the lattice at the side of the Hindu Temple (underneath the hanging serpentine forms) you can see the golden image of the Naga Sesa, Sesa Narayan. This temple is forbidden to non-Hindus and zealously guarded. Outside the door (to the right of the temple and to the left of the Guru Rinpoche Cave) is a stone image of Visnu's avatar Balarama (Stobs-ldan). (Chos-kyi Nyi-ma)

Since Chos-kyi Nyi-ma's time, the golden image of Sesa has disappeared and the temple is anything but well guarded. The image of Sesa

Narayan (Newari: Seg Narayan) is a garlanded wreath stone, painted fire-engine red to the right of the central image of Narayan. Sesa is 'The Remainder' of the cosmic ocean after Visnu has created the universe. He is identical to Visnu. Upon the dissolution of the universe he becomes Ananta, the Endless, upon which Visnu reclines at the end of his 'day'. Here the Naga is elevated to symbolise all Life Force, or the element water in its cosmic context where as the source of life it is pre-eminent. To the right of the temple are two stone friezes of Visnu's avatars, Balarama and Visnu Vikranta (Vamana). In Guru Rinpoche's Cave the Guru's hand holes and head print can be seen in the roof. This cave is usually occupied by a yogin associated with Guru Sangye Dorje's retreat centre, which is just to the north.

Ye-shes mTsho-rgyal visited Sakya De-ma (Sakya Devi), Jilajipha (Jilaji-sad), and others at Yanglesho and Asura during her first visit to Nepal (ca. 780-90). Sakya Dema was Guru Padma's mystic partner. (sTag-sham Nus-ldan rDo-rje) Her mother died at childbirth and she was left at the cremation ground after the cremation of her mother. She was reared by monkeys until Guru Padma discovered her and took her from Sankhu to Yanglesho to practise the Yang-dag and Phur-ba meditation rites. (Urgyan gLing-pa) When mTsho-rgyal met her she was a fully matured yogini in her own right and passed on the precepts, which she had received. (Urgyan gLing-pa)

28. PHARPING BAJRA JOGINI

Pham-thing rDo-rje rNal-`byor-ma: Pharping Bajra Jogini: this image of Vajra Yogini is the embodiment of pure awareness (Jnana, Ye-shes), and is a speaking Yogini. She is an image of the heart-vision of Pham-thing-pa and others.

"In the vicinity of Yanglesho is the Speaking Varahi of the Indian Pham-thing-pa." (Shing-kun dkar-chag)

"Close to the village of the Indian Pham-thing in a temple is an image of Vajra Yogini. This is Indra Khecari who defeats all opposition. However, her colour needs to be white while this image is red. Drukpa Rinpoche (the 6th `Brug-chen) told me that although this image was mde at a time of Pham-thing-pa it was restored and reconsecrated by a Buddhist Vajracarya at a later date." (Chos-kyi Nyi-ma)

Pham-thing Yogini, Uddhapada Yogini, Indra Yogini, or Nil Tara (to the Hindus), call her what you will, is red in colour with one foot firmly planted upon Mahesvara on the ground, while the other is raised straight into the sky pulled up by her left arm which presents a skull-cup to her mouth; a katvanga (a trident protruding from a skull on a stick) rests on her shoulder; and in her right hands she holds a hooked knife (gri-gug, kartika) slightly away from her side. To her right and left are Baghini and Singhini, the Tiger and Lion Headed Yoginis. Another three images with identical iconography are found in the northeast corner of the same first floor of the Bahal.

Chos-kyi Nyi-ma believed that the Nagaraj Sesa's epithet Phanathinggu, 'the Nine Hooded Cobra' had been corrupted into Pham-thing, which was then, in the 18th century, the name of the village or district, and that 'Indian' Pham-thing-pa took his name from his birthplace. Presumably, 'Pham-thing' has been corrupted into 'Pharping' according to this theory.[3] We can speculate that Pham-thing-pa gained his epithet 'Indian' from Indian ancestry or, more likely, from a prolonged sojourn in India itself. Or perhaps the Tibetans made no distinction between India and Nepal and called him 'Indian' Pham-thing-pa to distinguish him from Tibetans, because Pham-thing could be a Tibetan name. This great yogin of the Guhyasamaja, Sambara and Hevajra traditions was the spiritual son of Naropa who may have spent some time in the Kathmandu Valley.

Pham-thing-pa lived in the 11th century and was renowned as one of the great teachers of his day. He studied under Naropa for nine years, receiving the transmission of the Sambara and Hevajra-tantras amongst others. His brother Dus-'khorba studied under Naropa for five years and his youngest brother Thang-chung-pa was also a practising tantrika. (Blue Annals) Roerich adds that Pham-thing-pa was also known as Vagisvarakirti (Ngag-gi dbang-phyug grags-pa); that his remains are said to be preserved at Lo-chia-t'un in Kan-su where he died on his return from the Five Peaked Mountain Paradise of Manjusri (Wut'ai shan); and that pilgrims visit the village of Phambi (Pharping) near Kathmandu where descendants of Pham-thing-pa live.

29. ASURA CAVE

Asura-yi- brag-phug: Gorshanatha Gupha (Gorakhnath's Cave): in the upper meditation cave of Yanglesho, rDo-rje Phur-ba (Vajrakilaya) destroyed obstacles and obstructing spirits (in the meditation of Guru Padma) who gained mahamudra-siddhi there. This place possesses the blessings of supreme Buddha speech.

"In the upper meditation cave of Yanglesho I began the process of becoming aware of Glorious Yang-dag Heruka in order to obtain the relative powers and the ultimate compassion of mahamudra. But the suffering of the people of India and Nepal became such an obstacle to the consummation of my meditation that I begged my Gurus for the means to allay the people's suffering. The text of the Phur-ba Vitotama was sent me. Immediately after it arrived in Nepal the obstacles to my sadhana's progress were removed, and I attained the relative and ultimate compassion of mahamudra." (Orgyan mChog-'gyur gLing-pa) Guru Padma's practice in Yanglesho is a virtual precis of the Zangs-gling-ma description [see Yanglesho]. It seems most likely that Guru Padma performed his mahamudra retreat in the Asura Cave, the Upper Cave of Meditation of Yanglesho, as the lower cave near Sesa Narayan Sthan appears geomantically ill-placed for a prolonged retreat, it being entirely shaded by the crags above it and trees around it, and very damp, facing north, never receiving the light of the sun. However, although the texts are ambiguous and in conflict, it should not be dismissed that he practised in the lower cave.

"This is the place where (Guru Padma) accepted the pledges of the Twelve bStan-ma to protect Tibet: with regard to the Tantric rites of the rNying-ma School, on the occasion of protecting the essence of the teaching,/ In coming hither from India/ Or going hence from Nepal,/ In the Asura Cave/ The Master Padma `Byung-gnas/ And gLang-chen dPal-gyi Seng-ge/ Upon the yantra Throne of the Ten Spheres (Zhing-chen snol-pa'i gdan)/ An offering of 'red water' (blood) was prepared / And the vajra was turned in the hand;/ The secret initiatory name was uttered/ And they [the demons] were absorbed in the level of Vajradhara. Thus the description in ritual terms of the subjection of spirits, which Guru Padma performed not only in Yanglesho but in all parts of Tibet before beginning the building of Samye and attempting to convert the Bon-po Shamans to the Buddhist dharma. This is also the place where in the past many of the greatest of siddhas coming to and from India, Nepal and Tibet on foot would celebrate the Ganacakra rites and other pujas." (Chos-kyi Nyi-ma)

The name of the spirits called Phur-srung (Phur-ba Protectors), subjugated by Guru Padma at Asura, is significant in its implication that the phur-ba was an important local spiritual force. (Dudjom Rinpoche, Yid-kyi mun-sel: 40b)

"I have heard Drukpa Rinpoche (the 6th `Brug-chen) say that in the eye of a Knowledge Holder there is an entrance to the path which leads to the realm of the Asuras (anti-gods) from here, so that (by a yogin entering their realm) the Suras and Asuras can be converted." (Chos-kyi Nyi-ma)

"The Hindus have made this place into a power place of Visnu; but inside the small cave shaped like a lion there is no image of the god whatsoever. However outside the door is a horizontal stone, and carved in that stone are the complete set of Visnu's symbols, his footprints, his cakra and sword etc." (Chos-kyi Nyi-ma)

In the Asura cave are images of Guru Padma, Yang-dag Heruka and rDo-rje Phur-ba. In the rock above your head as you enter is a bulge seemingly about to split open: the story has it that quite recently a yogin was on the point of discovering one of the many Hidden Treasures (gter-ma) concealed by Guru Padma in the Asura Cave, when realising that the time was not auspicious for the disclosure of this secret, he broke his meditation, and the rock, which was about to break and give up its treasure, regained its intractability.

Outside, to the left of the entrance, is the handprint of Gorakhnath; and, likewise, the footprints in the rock in front of the entrance are said by some to be those of Gorakhnath. At some distance below the cave is a pitha of Ganes where the Remover of Obstacles can be seen struggling to free himself from the rock, while to his right is a small, exquisite self manifested image of Tara. In the cliff behind the cave the magical mineral jong-zhi can be found. This semi-crystallised form of calcium is employed in rasayana yogins' alchemical, dietary sadhana, and also by naturopathic and ayurvedic healers.

30. DAKSIN KALI

Lha mo nag-mo (Mahakali: Dhakini Kali: this fearful cremation ground is close to Pharping. The practitioner of Severence' (gcod) will certainly find his ambiance here.

"To the southwest of the town of Patan, not far from Thankot, there is a terrifying, predatory image of Ma-gcig `dod-khams dbag-mo (Kamalokesvari, the One Mother Queen of the Sensual Realm) called Daksina Kali." (bLa-ma bTsan-po)

Daksin Kali is the 'Southern Kali'. There are four principal Kalis in the Valley according to the classical Hindu lists: Vatsala, Mahakali, Daksin Kali and Guyhakali. Daksin Kali is patroness of the village of Pharping, but the most popular object of blood sacrifice in the entire Valley. The main shrine by the river is forbidden to non-Hindus; on the hillside above it is the site of a dhuni and the temple in which Tibetans pay homage.

31. KATOWA

Dang-po chu-bshar-ba'i gnas (the place of the first gorge): Katowa: south of Pharping is the place where Manjughosa caused the water [of the original lake] to drain away.

The Katowa gorge is where the River Bagmati breaks through the Sivalik range, a range rising to 8000' that separates Kathmandu Valley from India and is responsible for its cultural isolation and moderate monsoon.

32. THE BOUDHNATH STUPA

mChod-rten bya-rung-kha-shor (Chorten Jarung Khashor): Bahuda: a long time ago Jadzimo (Bya-rdzi-mo) and her four sons built this stupa with money saved from their wages. When the stupa was consecrated 100 million Buddhas dissolved into it, and it has the glory of being filled with their sacred relics (ring-bsrel). Whatever prayer is offered to it is fulfilled, and if you meditate upon your personal deity (yi-dam) here, at the time of your death you will be reborn in Sukhavati. Here is the cremation ground Spontaneously Amassed (Lhungrub brtsegs-pa), one of the Eight Great Cremation Grounds.

The Tibetans call the Boudhnath Stupa simply Chorten, The Stupa, or Chorten Chempo, the Great Stupa, or Jarung Khashor. This last name refers to the legend of its origin, which is related in the Padma bKa'-thang and also, at much greater length, in a gter-ma discovered by Rig-'dzin Yol-mo-pa Sakya-bzang-po in 1518. This revealed text, called The Legend of the Great Stupa (mChod-rten-chen-po bya-rung kha-shor-gyi lo-rgyus), tells the story of the whore who wounded the pride of the wealthy and powerful by building a magnificent monument to the Buddha with, of course, the king's permission. When the jealous lords petitioned the king to have the Stupa demolished, the king replied that once authority to build has been given it cannot be rescinded, which is the implied meaning of 'Jarung Khashor' (bya-rung kha-shor). But the story is related in Samye by Guru Padma who is asked by King Khri-Srong lDe-btsan to tell him and the other disciples what the fruit of the aspiration of the builders of the Jarung Khashor Stupa was.

And by relating the prayers of the benefactor Jadzima's sons, the past rebirths of the principal actors in the drama of spreading the Doctrine in Tibet - Guru Padma, the King, Santaraksita and sBa gSal-snang is described. When these four meet in Nepal and Tibet, their encounters are described as reunions. Two chapters in the gter-ma are devoted to prophecy, predictions concerning Tibet in general and the Great Stupa in particular. Guru Padma foresees the ruin of the Stupa and its restoration by a tulku who fulfils certain spiritual qualifications. According to Chos-kyi Nyi-ma this tulku is none other than Sakya-bzang-po himself who in the 16th century discovered the Stupa in ruins and undertook to restore it to its original state of glory. In 1505 he contributed wealth for the restoration of Swayambhu (Shing-kun dkar-chag). Again, according to Chos-kyi Nyi-ma, it was Sakya-bzang-po's third reincarnation, the gTer-ston bsTan-'dzin Nor-bu who propagated the doctrine he propounded in his first existence as a realised emanation of Guru Padma, that the Stupa was attached to the Spontaneously Amassed cremation ground, one of the Eight Great Cremation Grounds.

"It is written that [Jarung Khashor] is one of the eight stupas built at the Eight Great Cremation Grounds of the Eight Ma-mo (the Eight mother Goddesses, astamatrka) of Kala Bhairava's retinue when long ago Bhairava was vanquished by Cakrasambara... Not far from the Stupa is a cremation ground lake called Naga Talapa; on the banks of that is a cremation ground tree; very close to the Stupa is a cremation ground fire, that has remained alight for ever and a day, called Agamatha; and ordinary people have seen clouds of Dakinis from time to time in the vicinity of the Stupa. For these and other reasons this is described as a cremation ground stupa." (bLa-ma bTsan-po)

Possibly, the tree mentioned above is the bodhivrksa, the peepal tree, outside the main gate of Guhjeswori. Upstream from here is a broad lake bed to the north of the Bagmati. The fire, Agamatha, is perhaps the eternal fire of Sankhu Bajra Jogini.

"In the Spontaneously Amassed Cremation ground in Nepal dwells the blood-sucking serpent-witch Kasmali. Surrounding the stupa are funereal birds, sepulchral creatures, a cremation ground, ghouls brandishing skeletons, and creatures of the tombs. A flashing cloud of airy regions lifts heaps of men, fire, skins and pulverised organs; a Yaksa vomits tigers, wolves and other wild beats. Here Padma subdues the eight classes of demons, reduces the three worlds, subjugates the three domains, and turns the wheel of dharma for five years. Here he is known as Seng-ge sgra-sgrogs, He Who Teaches with a Lion's Roar." [Adapted from Urgyan gLing-pa: 176ff.]

"We definitely accept that the Protectress who is at the front side (the north side of the Stupa) is Puska, red and gold, sucking up entrails and devouring them, and that she is one of the Eight Ma-mo of this power place." (Chos-kyi Nyi-ma)

The Ma-mo (matrka) Puska or Kasmali (Urgyan gLing-pa), known also as Pukasi, is to be found in the shrine opposite the residence and shrine room of the Abbot of Boudha, the Chini Lama. She squats with a corpse on her knees devouring its intestines. She is treated with great respect by her devotees, most of whom are Bhotiyas, Tamangs and Tibetans, and therefore initiated into the Mandala of the Eight Ma-mo attendant upon the Cremation Ground. By the Newars she is known by the generic name Ajima (grandmother), a name applied particularly to the astamatrka but also to other fierce goddesses. Some Nepalis identify her with Haritima, a demoness who inflicted smallpox upon children until converted by Sakyamuni preaching the significance of Swayambhu at Puran Swayambhu (Vasubandhu's Stupa). Thereafter she fulfilled her vow to remain within here shrines that were located close to the Buddha's temples, and so long as she was propitiated she would refrain from inflicting disease. In Swayambhu, and likewise in Katisimbhu, she appears in her usual form of a benign mother with children on her knees. The Hindus call her Sitala. Camunda is the astamatrka of the Hindus who is depicted devouring a corpse' guts. Whatever her name this goddess is a force to propitiate to prevent her malicious devices infecting one rather than to coerce and employ her siddhi. Regmi agrees that the Boudhnath Stupa, otherwise called Khasti, has been associated with Bhotiyas from a very early time. He suggests that the name Khasti is derived from Khasa, a town near Kyirong inside Tibet (Regmi 1965, Pt. 1: 571). We know that in the 17th – 19th centuries the Tibetan government had some jurisdiction over the Stupa and that it has been, and is still, worshipped principally by Tamangs, Gurungs and other Bhotiyas. When the 13th Karmapa visited Nepal in 1723 he first paid homage to Boudhnath. The 6th Zhamarpa also went first to Boudha in his 1614 visit.

The Newars also call the Boudha Stupa Khas or Khasti, and their story of the Stupa's origin is quite different from that of the Tibetans. The implication of The Legend of the Great Stupa is that the Stupa had been built many generations before the birth of Guru Padma, Khri-Srong lDe-btsan and the others, in the dvapara-yuga at the time of Kasyapa, since his relics are of its birth date. The Newari story fixes the century of its foundation, the 6th century, because it was the great King Manadeva, the military conqueror and patron of the arts, whose deeds are recorded on the Changu Narayan pillar, who built it. Manadeva, one of the greatest Licchavi Kings, died in 505 A.D. (Regmi 1965).

During the reign of Vikramajit, the Narayana Hiti, the fountain opposite the old gate of the new palace, ran dry, and a drought struck the land. The King consulted his astrologers, and was informed that the gods required the death of a virtuous man, such propitiation being the only means to end the drought. The King searched his kingdom but discovered that only he and his son qualified as victims. The old king decided that he himself must die, and instructed his son to decapitate with one stroke the shrouded form that he found lying beside the Narayana Hiti on a certain moonless night. The son, Manadeva, obeyed his father's command, and was horrified to see the head of his own father fly up from the corpse and away in the at the Bajra Jogini Temple, where the Dakini told him that the only way to expiate his sin was to let fly a cock, and wherever the bird landed he should build a reliquary stupa for his father's remains. The cock alighted at Boudha. Some say that the Great Stupa itself is Manadeva's penitential monument; others that the largest of the five stupas to the east of the Great Stupa is Vikramajit's reliquary.

"On the east side of (Jarung Khaqsor) is a stupa enshrining the relics of Rang-rig-ras-pa." (Shing-kun dkar-chag) Rang-rig-ras-pa was a highly respected Lama of the bKa'-brgyud-pa school who lived in the 17th century. The Chini Lama believes that he was a Khams-pa, the 5th and last of his line of incarnations and that his remains were interred in the largest of the stupas on the east side. Chini Lama had a vision of Rang-rig-ras-pa who instructed him in tantric practice. The Chini Lama also believes that the second largest of the stupas to the east is the reliquary of rTogs-ldan Sakya Sri, the famous Lama active in western Tibet during the last century, who restored the Boudha Stupa at one time. Sakya Sri was the Guru of the late Abu Rinpoche's teacher.

33. CHABAHIL STUPA

Sa-lhag rdo-lhag-gi mchod-rten (the stupa of Earth and Stone Remnants): Cabhel ko cayite: this stupa was constructed from the gloriously consecrated earth and stone remnants of the Boudha Stupa.

The Chabahil Stupa is of great antiquity. The Newar tradition asserts that it was built by the Mauryan Emperor Dharma Asoka's daughter, Carumati, who stayed behind to marry a local prince when Asoka visited the Valley in the 3rd century B.C. Carumati's husband, Devapala, is credited with building Deopatan. A very early Licchavi inscription attests to the age of the site and an early Licchavi standing Buddha and a later Padmapani Lokesvara are important monuments to exquisite Licchavi craftsmanship. The name Manju Bahal indicates that in centuries past a Bahal existed around the Stupa; today the Stupa area is known as Bhagawan Than. To the west of the stupa is the Carumati Vihara of which Dipankara Buddha is the kwapa-deo. Regmi calls the Stupa Dhanju Caitya, perhaps a misreading of 'Manju' (Regmi 1965: 564)

34. GUHJESWORI

Phag-mo mngal-chu (Varahi's Womb-Fluid): Guhyashwori (Mistress of the Secret): the Stupa of Self-Sprung Wisdom, Swayambhu, appeared upon the pollen bed of a flower growing from the womb of Vajra Varahi; and because here is the root of Swayambhu, which is beautified by so many kinds of trees, this root is said to be the umbilical cord which nurtures Kathmandu. Beside [the Temple of Guhjeswori] flows the Bagmati, one of the four great rivers [of the Valley], the auspicious waters of which purify all sin and obscuration.

"Near Pasupati is a symbol of Uma called Guhjeswari where there is also a spring which has the taste and smell of chung (fermented grain liquor)." (bLa-ma bTsan-po)

In the central shrine of the temple complex are two circular wells with rims slightly raised above the floor. The largest and shallower well is employed in rites of worship as the symbol of Uma, the yoni, while the other well, supposedly 30' deep, and smaller in diameter, is the receptacle of chung, arak and red powdered water (blood or a substitute) offered in worship. A spring overflows onto the temple floor from this well, as outflow that is considered to be the sexual nectar of the Yogini-Goddess herself.

"On the banks of the Vakmati (Bagmati), the gSung-ldan-ma, is Guhyasvari (Sanskrit), which means the Secret Goddess, (gSang-ba'i dbang-phyug, where 'Secret' means 'Private' as in 'Private parts'), a sound that has been corrupted so that both Indians and Nepalis pronounce it Gutiswari (The Rectum Goddess or Hidden Goddess), and thus the Tibetan's say 'Varahi's Womb-Fluid' (Phag-mo mngal-chu)." (Chos-kyi Nyi-ma)

These days the Nepalis pronounce it Guhjeswori. The ambiguity of the name is compounded by the Hindu legend of Sati; it was the anus or rectum [guda) of Sati's corpse that fell here while Siva was flying around the sub-continent insane with grief, allowing parts of the decomposing corpse of his beloved wife to fall at the Sakta pithasthanas. However, it is clear that at Guhjeswori the Buddhists worship the 'lotus' as a symbol of Vajra Varahi, red in colour, the Consort of Cakrasambara, or as Nairatma (bDag-med-ma), blue in colour, the Consort of Hevajra. Guhjeswori is also the Bird Headed Dakini [see Pasupati]. In the tantra and iconography of the Four Dakinis as found the Bidjeswori Bahal, Guhjeswori is the Two Headed Vajra Varahi. The Hindus worship the yoni as the symbol of Uma and Parvati, the Consort of Siva and Bhairav. Karmacarya Srestha priests are the custodians of the shrine and strictly enforce the exclusion of non-Hindus.

The lotus seed thrown by Vipaswi Buddha from Nagarjuna Hill fell at this spot, and from that seed bloomed the vast lotus upon which the magical flame of the Swayambhu Dharmadhatu shone forth. After the lake was drained, Manjusri, inspecting the lake bottom, discovered the root of this lotus, and having received a visitation of Guhyesvari, he built the first shrine to her in the form of a triangular yantra. Then he covered the root, and taking earth and stone from Guhjeswori he made the first support for the Swayambhu Lotus (Swayambhu Purana).

35. PASUPATI

Lha-chen dbang-phyug-gi gnas (the Power Place of Lhachen Wongchuk-Mahadeva Isvara): Pasupati Sthan: Mahadeva came from the realm of the gods (Kailas) and established this residence called Gu-lang [by the Tibetans]. A bull manifest in stone can be found there, and nearby is the path to hell and other marvels.

"In the middle of the town of Gu-lang is Pasupati, the Lord of the Beasts, a self-manifest lingam of Mahesvara with four faces within an extremely beautiful pagoda style temple full of all kinds offerings. To one side of the temple is an iron trisul as high as a two-storied house. Since blood sacrifice is made to both Gutiswari and Pasupati, they are both very terrible gods. It is said that long ago the siddha Jalandharipa (Gorakhnath's Guru) revealing his psychic energy, burst the Pasupati lingam apart through magical means. Unquestionably that was supposed to have occurred here, but I do not know whether the lingam is actually cracked or broken because it is covered and obscured by many ornaments and one is not permitted to go close to it. However, making the necessary enquiries as to whether the Pasupati lingam is the original self-manifest symbol or a substitute, nowadays some people will say that the Siddha's curse destroyed it long ago and that at a certain time it was put into a wooden Buddhist stupa, so that, covered up, it was preserved. Whatever happened, this power place is immensely famous, and each year at a certain time of a certain month (Marg krsna 13) a very large number of Indian people congregate to perform worship (on Mahasivaratri). This custom is still very much alive." (Chos-kyi Nyi-ma)

"East of Kathmandu and between Kathmandu and Bhaktapur is the village of Debapatan (Deopatan) and this place is numbered among the Twenty Four Great Power Places as the northern spoke of the Wheel of Buddha Body (sKu'i dkyil-`khor) called Grihadebada (Grhadeva), or, as it is more widely known from the Sri Hevajra-maharajatantra, Naipala. The Pasupatiswara lingam, which is raised as a symbol for worship of Mahadeva, who is protector of the land of the Nepalis, is called Gu-lang by the Tibetans." (bLa-ma bTsan-po)

In the Cakrasambara-tantra and in the kLong-chen sNyig-thig tradition Grhadeva is listed amongst the 24 pithasthanas as the external reference symbolic of the anus, or the anal nerve, in the Yogin's identification with the Dakini, and as the northern spoke of the Wheel of the Buddha's Body. Sati's anus or rectum landed at Guhjeswori.

Chos-kyi Nyi-ma affirms that the essential mark of a great power place is a spontaneously arisen lingam and yoni (Swayambhu lingam and yoni), and since both Pasupati and Guhjeswori possess these self-manifest symbols, like Ti-se (Kailas) and Pretapuri Tsaritra (Tsa-ri) in Tibet, they are indeed the heart of the paradise upachandoha (yul-chen-po nye-ba'i tshandoha) that is the Kathmandu Valley. However, Chos-kyi Nyi-ma continues, while the exotericists understand the gross symbolism of the lingam and yoni as the passive and active symbols of power, and worship them as Mahadeva and Uma (or Parvati) and are their slaves, the esotericists understand the ultimate nature of the symbols and worship that as Sri Cakrasambara and Vajra Varahi in indissoluble union (yab-yum) and so control Mahadeva and Uma (this is a nice non-sectarian interpretation, as surely the Nath yogins, for instance, are esotericists). The Buddhist tantrika who takes refuge in the symbol rather than its absolute reality breaks his SAMAYA. Thus Guhjeswori must be realised to be either the Vagina of Vajra Varahi or the Dakini Queen, the Bird-Headed Yogini (one of Cakrasambara's protecting yoginis) who is the spirit of the earth, a dance of thoroughly enjoyable material illusion, accompanied by her vast retinue (sa-la spyod-pa'i dpa'mo'i dbang-phyug bya-gdong-ma 'khor grangs-med-pa). In mythological terminology, in the distant past, long ago, Canda Bhairav and Uma projected themselves as their lingam and yoni symbols into the 24 pithasthanas. Later, Glorious Heruka Yab-yum, Cakrasambara and Vajra Varahi, with their boundless retinue arrived at these power places and vanquished the god and goddess, blessing the lingam and yoni as themselves. (Chos-kyi Nyi-ma) In metaphysical terminology, the fundamental, dualistic principles of existence, Siva-sakti, passive and active, male and female, are dominated and controlled by the realisation of the essential Emptiness (Sunyata) of all phenomena, and in the consequent unitary reality, passivity becomes skilful means (upaya) and activity becomes insight (prajna) - compassion (Heruka) and wisdom (Varahi) coincident (yuganadha). In historical terms, to infer from this passage that Saivism preceded Buddhism into Tantra (it probably did not) would be an overly simplistic interpretation. But the ancient orthodox Saivite and the Sakta cults were in existence when the siddhas popularised the Sambara and other Buddhist tantras. Thus the Sambara sadhaka would utilise the already existing facilities as the 24 (or 108) power places (pithasthanas). Further, we may surmise that the geomantic qualities of these pithas had marked them from time immemorial as focil for all hues and persuasions of rishis, yogins and contemplatives, the majority of whom were not Buddhist monks.

In answer to Chos-kyi Nyi-ma's question as to whether the present Pasupati lingam is the original image or the one broken by Jalandharipa (whose name derives from the pitha of Jalandhara, Mandi, Himachal Pradesh, India), an inscription at Pasupati records the consecration of a new image to replace that broken into three parts by the Muslims in their 14th century invasion (see Regmi 1965, Pt. 1: 316). Regmi also claims that the original 3rd century lingam lies amidst ruins close to the sanctuary. I have been unable to confirm this.

Chos-kyi Nyi-ma used the name Gu-lang to describe the village of Deopatan which surrounds the Pasupati shrine and which was built by the Emperor Dharma Asoka's son-in-law. Others call Pasupatinath himself Gu-lang. In Tibet Gu-lang was a deity who blessed women with conception, a boon often begged of Pasupati by local women.

The four faced lingam (caturmukha-lingam) is said to suppress Siva's jyotir-lingam, the endless pillar of fire Siva projected so that in the contest between Visnu and Brahma to find the height and depth of it, Brahma could falsely claim that he had reached the top, thus proving himself unworthy of worship. As proof of the tolerance in Newari religion, the four faces of the caturmukha-lingam of Pasupatinath are generally believed to represent Siva, Surya, Visnu and Buddha. Orthodox Brahmins, however, believe that the four faces represent the four vedas.

The path to hell is said by local people to begin at a door in the cliff between Arje Ghat and Surje Ghat, or on the flank of the hill Kailas Parbat near a sadhu's kuti (meditation hut) where a spiral stairway descends to a brick wall. Overly zealous Buddhists say that it exists only in the minds of atmavadins.

36. TILOPA AND NAROPA'S CAVES

Telopa'i phug-pa: Arje Ghat Ganeshsthan (Arya Ghat): here [Manjughosa] cut a third gorge. Later it became known for Telopa and Naropa's Cave.

Two hundred yards up river from Pasupatinath, on Surje Ghat (Surya Ghat) are the two siddhas' caves, among others, carved out of the living rock. The river cuts through a ridge that would have contained a lake spreading east beyond Sankhu.

Arje Ghat is immediately below the Pasupati Shrine; this is the ghat upon which the Kings of Nepal, Pasupatinath's principal votaries, are cremated. Ganesthan is a few yards down stream and enshrines seven images of Ganapati.

37. CHOBAR GORGE

Cowar: the second gorge was cut at Chobar on the road to Taudah Lake.

On the west side of the gorge are several meditation caves. An enclosed overhang forms a kuti where Gorakhnath himself (or one of his lineage) is reputed to have meditated. Rwa Lotsawa is also said to have meditated in one of these caves. Behind the caves is a labyrinth of tunnels that penetrate to an underground lake. There are no images within. One of the tunnels that are now bricked up leads up to the Adinath Temple of Karunamaya/Machhendranath in the Co Bahal of Chobar Village high on the ridge. Ganes dug it after he had been omitted from a meeting of the gods at the Bahal. Leaving his Jalavinayaka residence of the south end of the gorge, he arrived enraged at the centre of the convocation and demanded an explanation of the slight.

Rwa Lotsawa rDo-rje grags-pa (Rwa-lo) was one of the luminaries of the phyi-dar, the later spreading of the dharma in Tibet. He came to Nepal to receive initiation from 'Ba'-ro (probably Bharo, an honorific title) who gave him the Vajra Varahi and Vajra Bhairava transmissions. 'Ba'-ro lived in the Nyi-ma stong (Thousand Suns) Vihara in Patan. Rwa-lo defeated the heaviest of 300 Hindu yogins at Swayambhu; and he did puja and meditation at Yanglesho, Jarungkhashor, Godavari, Tsha-ba tsha-shod (Gung-thang), Namo Buddha, Manicura and Swayambhu. This was in the 11th century. (Rwa-lotsawa rnam-thar)

38. GOKARNA

The fourth gorge was cut at Kokarna on the road to Yalmo and one league from the Boudha Stupa.

39. CHEMCHOK HERUKA

Che-mchog Heruka (the Supreme Sovereign Heruka): Bisorup: this image is found at Gu-lang (Pasupati).

Visorup is enshrined in a temple courtyard two hundred yards east of the Sivapuri Kailas complex on the hill between Pasupati and Guhjeswori. The central image is of Visnu Visvarupa; but since Visvarupa is taken by Buddhists to express the universal, manifest, inchoate form of divinity, the deity is conceived of in various ways. Thus the Tibetans worship this image as Che-mchog, and some Bhutanese as the Thousand Armed Avalokitesvara (Thugs-rje-chen-po dug lnga rang-grol). Chemchog is one of Guru Padma's sGrubs-pa bKa'-brgyad Deities.

"To the south of Boudhnath is... Orgyen's Throne and his sadhana spring." (Shing-kun dkar-chag) The exact location of the Lhun-grub-brtsegs-pa Cremation Ground where Guru Padma of Orgyen was transmogrified into Senge sGra-sgrogs is not known. Chos-kyi Nyi-ma mentions a cremation ground tree with an image of Gorakhnath in its vicinity; this could possibly be the tree near the nath yogins' akara in Sivapuri Kailas, or, alternatively, the tree outside the Che-mchog Temple. It is likely that the Che-mchog shrine is Orgyen's Throne.

40. MANICURA THAN

Grub-thob brgyad-cu'i gnas (The Power Place of the Eighty Siddhas): Manicuta sthan: the place where the righteous king Manicura (gTsug-na Nor-bu) made a gift of his jewel, and the power place of the Eighty Siddhas, is called Manilinga, the jewel that was sawed off (from his head). You will see many bathers in the river.

"To the north of Sankhu is a place blessed by the Eighty Siddhas." (Shing-kun dkar-chag)

"I have heard that in the neighbourhood of Sankhu is a cave of the Eighty Four Mahasiddhas, and images etc." (bLa-ma bTsan-po)

"On the top of the mountain behind (Sankhu Bajra Jogini) is what is known as Manilinga. The name of the mountain is 'Jewel Pile' (Nor-bu brtsegs-pa'i ri, Manicur Dara), and long ago on this peak the Bodhisattva Manicuda (Nor-bu'i gtsug), after sitting in samadhi for a very long time, cut off his jewelline jata (the protuberance that emerges from a Buddha's fontanelle at enlightenment) on one occasion; this offering turned into stone, and it is now called Manilinga (Jewel Phallus). Further, not far away from the Manilinga is a waterfall called Maniloha (Bloody Jewel), because blood which poured forth from the Bodhisattva's crown when he performed his great act of generosity mingled with the waters there." (Chos-kyi Nyi-ma)

There is no single cave here in which the 84 Mahasiddhas gathered; there are four of five caves located between the top of the Manicura Dara and Sankhu Bajra Jogini in which, over the centuries, many siddhas both Tibetan and Indian practised their meditation. The cave of Nagarjuna, close to Bajra Jogini, contains an image of the Master. Sankaracarya, the arch rival of Dharmakirti, lived in a cave here, and Chos-kyi Nyi-ma claims to have heard many stories about his stay from Indians; the Nepalis also have many legends of his association with Nepal, and particularly Sankhu. There is a Ye-shes mTsho-rgyal Cave near Bajra Jogini, but Sankhu is not mentioned in mTsho-rgyal's biography. In Peking, Lama bTsan-po was informed that there was a cave of Pha Dam-pa Sangs-rgyas, wherein the saint had left his hand

and foot prints and where there was an image of him, located near Camkhu, which could be either Changu Narayan or Sankhu. No doubt at least 84 siddhas have practised their meditation in this area.

The legend of the Buddha Sakyamuni's previous rebirth as King Manicuda is told in the Newari text Manicudavadanoddhrta, which is probably based on the account of Ksemendra in the Sanskrit Bodhisattvavadankalpalata. The King Manicuda was born into the royal family of Saket (Ayodhya in north India) and after he assumed the throne he became the model Bodhisattva monarch. Indra, to test him, transformed himself into a Raksasa and demanded that the King feed him. Scorning human food the Raksasa insisted upon the King's flesh, which Manicuda gave him without stint. Later on he gave his beautiful and loving wife and her son to a rsi who begged them in order to offer them to his Guru as the fee for learning. Then Manicuda abandoned the world, and was carried by two pratyekabuddhas to the Himalayas where he began to practice yoga and meditation. But still dissatisfied, wishing to attain enlightenment, the King sought an opportunity to give his body as an ultimate gesture in his practice of generosity. When five Brahmins appeared and asked for the jewel in his head to take to their plague-afflicted country, so that the water in which it was bathed could cure the diseased, Manicuda felt himself most fortunate and instructed the Brahmins to cut out the jewel. The stone on which the King's head was cut open was covered with blood, and the stream into which the blood flowed was called Manirohini. Indra healed the King's wounds with the remedy samjivani, the rsis paid him homage, and a jewel twice as bright as the one he had give away appeared in his head. After his body had been restored to its previous wholeness, his queen and son arrived at his mountain fastness to beg him to return to his kingdom, and upon the advice of the pratyekabuddhas he again took up the reins of government. (See Lienhard: 1963).

41. SANKHU BAJRA JOGINI

gSangs-gu kya (?) rnal-`byor-ma: Sakhu Bajra Jogini: with the radiance of mKha'-spyod remaining (mKha'-spyod gdongs bzhugs), here is an extraordinary, sublime image of Yogini, and an eternal flame.

"Just off the road from gNya'-nang to the Kathmandu Valley is a village called Sankhu Bajra Dakini, which is known to the Hindus as Sankhu Narayani, where there is an image of the venerable Vajra Dakini which gives extraordinarily powerful blessing." (bLa-ma bTsan-po)

"The chief symbol of this power place is the Goddess Ugratara, or Ekajati, inside a pagoda temple with a gilt copper roof. She is red in colour with one face and four arms, two of which hold a skull-cup (kapala) and knife (karpatra) at her heart, and the remaining two hold a sword (khadga) and an utpala lotus. In the upper temple is an identical image of Ugratara in bell metal, in which her left leg is outstretched (in pratyalida?); to the left and right of her is a hollow copper vessel and the head of Bintiraja... In the upper temple is the loom of the Nepali Princess Bhrkuti... In another room is a stone Swayambhu Stupa. I know neither the builder nor the dates of these artefacts. Both Buddhists and Hindus have their separate tantras and sadhanas of Ugratara. She is accounted as a superior goddess of wisdom (Shes-rab-kyi lha). The Hindus perform blood sacrifice to her. There is reputed to be an eternal fire and an eternal spring here." (Chos-kyi Nyi-ma)

"In the Kathmandu Valley Padma Sambhava did pilgrimage to Sankhu where he met Sakya Devi and took here to Yanglesho [p.315]... Vairotsana, leaving Tibet after his dharma was slandered, stopped in Nepal and offered a golden icon to the monastery of Sankhu [p.454]... In the monastery of Sankhu and other Nepali monasteries... and other places round about, [Guru Padma] hid one thousand other treasures [p.365]." (Urgyan gLing-pa) According to the Newari tradition, the Sankhu Bajra Jogini is the elder of the four sister yoginis of the Valley - Sankhu Khadga Jogini, Guhjeswori, Pham-thing Jogini and Bidjeswori. Since she is associated with Manicuda [q.v.] she is called Mani Jogini; since she holds a blue utpala lotus in her left hand she is called Nil Tara (?); since the sword is her distinctive emblem, she is popularly known as Khadga Jogini; though she is of serene mien she is Ugratara, Tara in angry mood, according to the Buddhist tantra; because here iconography is commensurate with the Goddess Protectresses and she is a form of Durga (Sankhu Narayani: Narayani is a name of the matrka Vaisnavi or Visnusakti, the Consort of Visnu, i.e. Durga), Chos-kyi Nyi-ma calls her Ekajati. The Hindus also count her among the Dasamahavidhya (the ten aspects of the Mother Goddess's wisdom) where she is worshipped as the personification of spiritual hunger. But the Hindu tradition acknowledges that she was originally a Buddhist deity, and even today a Hindu Guru will direct his chela to practise ritual meditation according to the Buddhist liturgy.

When Sankaracarya, or one of his ardent disciples, was living in Sankhu, there was conflict with the followers of the Buddhas' path. Ugratara's necklace of skulls (mundamala) is composed of the heads of

Sankaracarya's Brahmin followers. The sword that she carries was borrowed from her younger sister, Guhjeswori, (where did Guhjeswori keep this sword?), in fulfilment of Sankaracarya's petition after he had been humbled by her for arrogantly upturning a swayambhu stupa to demonstrate his power to his Brahmin followers. The blood in her kapala is the blood of Brahma collected when she severed his head at the behest of a reluctant Mahadev after Brahma had lost his contest with Vishu to discover the height and depth of Siva's jyotir lingam.

In both the upper and lower temples, Yogini is flanked by Baghini and Singhini, the Tiger and Lion-headed Yoginis. In the same upper room in the upper temple is a solid bronze standing Buddha and a standing Lokeswar. Below this shrine room is a small room containing a swayambhu stupa flanked by a Buddha's head, which is known as the head of Vikramajit (or Vrsadeva) who Chos-kyi Nyi-ma 's Bintiraja, the parricide Manadeva's father (see Boudhnath), and an upturned frying-pan to which is attached an irrational moral legend. The casting of the bronze figures is reputed to be of outstanding quality (see Slussor 1974).

Indisputably, Sankhu Bajra Jogini is one of the Valley's oldest shrines. There is the 5th century association with Manadeva; an Amsuvarman inscription of the 7th century mentions a Gum Vihara which may be identified with the Gvam Vihara of Bajra Jogini (Regmi 1965: 278); Urgyan gLing-pa's Padma bKa'-thang mentions Sankhu three times in the history of the 8th century; Sankaracarya may have visited in the 9th century However, there is a mystery associated with Bajra Jogini herself. Tara was originally a Buddhist deity, but in her Sankhu form the Gvam Vihara Licchavi Buddhist bronze casters would never have worshipped her. If we discount the legend associated with Sankaracarya [see above], it would seem possible that a long time before the present temple was built by Raja Prakas Malla in 1655, the site was usurped by Hindu priests who established the Devi as the chief image (kwapa-deo) for worship and instituted blood sacrifice to her. A devi pitha is an unlikely site for the establishment of a hinayana vihara and blood sacrifice is never performed for Buddhist yoginis. Today, Buddhist Newar priests again attend the temple, and blood is shed at the Bhairabi pitha below. If the name Bajra Jogini has a Buddhist provenance, and a Buddhist goddess was in power in the 9th century, it is unlikely that she was Ugratara, perhaps she was a different deity, such as Naro Khecari (Naropa's Dakini), who of the four yogini's associated with the Cakrasambara-tantra, is the only one without a sthan of her own. More research into this very interesting shrine is necessary.

42. CANGU NARAYAN

Khyung rang-byon (the Self-Manifest Garuda): Cangu Narayana than: this Garuda is generally believed to have grown out of Arya Nagarjuna's rosary. It is highly praised for the relief of Naga-related diseases.

"At Changu (Chang-khung) there is a self-manifest Garuda holding a Naga before it." (Shing-kun dkar-chag)

"In the middle of a large town (grong-khyer) that in Newari is called Cang-khung and by the Tibetans corrupted to Sa-'go is a elf-manifest Garuda. The story concerning the emergence of this Garuda from Nagarjuna's rosary is well known in Tibet." The legend known to Indians and Nepalis is that this Garuda (mKa'-lding), the vehicle of Visnu, is self-manifest from a gigantic ruby (Padmaraga), and its name is Garuda Narayan, or the 'Garuda Self-manifest from a Jewel'. Furthermore, in summertime here, a real Garuda appears from gathering rainclouds and picks a Naga out of the Sankhadaha lake (below), and anyone can see the Garuda devour the Naga. At this time, in the temple, the image of Garuda perspires, and many people come here to moisten scarves with the exuding perspiration to gain protection from the ravages of Naga spirits. It is said that last year (i.e. some time in the middle of the 18th century) when an invading army was threatening the Valley, the image of Garuda Narayan was taken to the King's palace in Kathmandu and a replica set up in its place. Anyhow, the present image is of gilt copper. (Chos-kyi Nyi-ma)

Leprosy is the most dangerous disease inflicted by the Nagas; also abscesses, consumption, ulcers, itch, sores and swelling of the limbs, and all diseases related to excessive indulgence, or lack of the element water.

Cangu Narayan is located between the Sankhu road and Bhaktapur. It is one of the oldest sites in the Valley. A pillar inscription of Manadeva (dated 464) records his 5th century exploits. The Garuda, or the replica that is held to be so sacred, is found within the central temple. Another Garuda, with hands held in prayer, found in front of the temple, is believed to have the face of Manadeva and is certainly of great antiquity. Some of the Valley's best stone sculpture is to be found at Cangu Narayan.

43. BHAKTAPUR DIPANKARA

Kho-khom sangs-rgyas mar-me-mdzad: Bhadgha'um Dipamkara: in Bhaktapur you will see many images of Dipankara and the Five Buddha Aspects (rigs-lnga) etc.

There are five Dipankara Brothers in Bhaktapur: in Jhaurabhai (mangala Dharmadvipa Vihara), in Tadhunchen Bahal (Caturvarna Mahavihara), in Kothubhai, in Tatubhai (Sayakirti Mahavihara), and the principal of the five that Tibetans were in the habit of visiting is called Ajudyo and is found in the Adibuddha Vihara in Kwatandau. During Ganla on Panchadan the five Dipankaras visit Laska Deo (see Bhaktapur Lokeswara), their younger sister (bahini), and present her with a tola of gold.

44. BHAKTAPUR TALKING TARA

sGrol-ma gsung-byon (Talking Tara): Bolne Tara: this is the Talking Tara who told the King of Bhaktapur to invite the venerable Milarepa to the city. It is found in the palace.

"In Bhaktapur is the Talking Tara (sGrol-ma gsung-byung-ma), exceedingly great in blessings." (Shing-kun dkar-chag)

The Taleju Temple complex in Bhakatpur Palace is closed to non-Hindus, and a mystery surrounds the nature of the images within. It is evident, however, that it was not the Taleju image that was brought from Ayodhya in 1323 by Hara Singha Deva fleeing from the Muslim Tuklak Shah who spoke to the Bhaktapur King in the late 11th or early 12th centuries. Yet this Taleju image subsequently became the protecting Deity of Bhaktapur and later of all Nepali Kings, and is believed to take pride of place in the agama-che (the secret shrine) of the palace temple complex. I have heard it said that there is an image of Green Tara in this agama-che, and if this is true then this must be the older deity who spoke of Milarepa. The most likely king to have sent an invitation to Milarepa is Hasadeva (ca. 1090-1097), or perhaps Sivadeva (ca. 1101-1123) or Singhadeva (ca. 1111-1121), the last two kings ruling concurrently.

According to local informants there are other Talking Taras in Bhaktapur.

45. BHAKTAPUR SAKYAMUNI

Shakya thub mgon: Bhagawan: this image is to be found in the Sakyamuni Vihara in Bhaktapur.

The Bhaktapur Sakyamuni visited by Tibetans is to be found in Jhaurbhai (Mangala Dharmadvipa Vihara) in Golinadhitol. The central image (kwapa-deo) is Sakyamuni in dhyanamudra. One of the five Dipankaras also resides here.

46. BHAKTAPUR LOKESWARA

sPyan-ras-gzigs: Lokeswara than: this is in Bhaktapur.

The principal Bhaktapur Lokeswara is Laska Deo, otherwise known as Annapurna Lokeswara, who is to be found in the Marilachen Temple of Itachentole. He is an image of Padmapani Avalokitesvara, and is also known as Rato Matsyendranath like his brother in Patan.

47. NYISHANG KURTI

gNye-shang kurti: Bagishwari Saraswati Sthan: this is a mile and a half from the long guest house, and is the place where the venerable Milarepa meditated.

"At Nyishang Gurta in Mon, (Milarepa) met Repa the Hunter (Khyi-ras-pa). It was he who spread the renown of the Master in Nepal. Prompted by a message from the Goddess Tara the King of Bhaktapur (Kho-khom) honoured the Master." (gTsang-myon: 150).

In The Hundred Thousand Songs of Milarepa two chapters relate stories of Tibet's Great Yogi in Nyishang. Milarepa is meditating in a cave on the Nyi-shang Gurda Mountain when a deer appears and drops exhausted at Mila's feet. Immediately afterwards the hunting dog that had been chasing it appears and also lies down in peace and contentment. Finally, the hunter (Khyi-ra-pa) is converted by Milarepa and given the name Khyi-ras-pa (Chirepa). This vignette is illustrated in the popular thang-ka showing Milarepa sitting in front of cave with his hand to his ear, surrounded by deer, dog and hunter. The second story finds Mila meditating in the same cave, the Gurdaya Cave ('the cave of Nyishang on the Gadaya Mountain in Mon'), where he is physically abused by local hunters. Unable to break his samadhi, though they throw him into a river gorge, their contempt changes to devotion and respect. Mila's fame reaches the ear of the King of Kathmandu and Bhaktapur who prompted by the Talking Tara invites him to the palace. The Master declines the King's invitation with a homily on the virtues of the ascetic life. (Mila mGur-bum Ch. 26 & 27: 275 ff.)

"In gNyi-shang kurti is the residence of rJe-btsun bZhad-pa rDo-rje, and here Khyi-ra-pa mGon-po rDo-rje was converted and became his disciple. The footprints of a deer are to be found clearly marked in a rock. The fame of rJe-btsun-chen-po's name spread widely in Nepal where he is known as Hasa Vajra, and in a detailed biography, unknown to me, are his famous songs and utterances, some of which are translated into Sanskrit and sung. To the Newars this power place is known as Vagiswari." (Chos-kyi Nyi-ma)

'The long guest house' remains unidentified. Nyishang Kurti and the nearby Saraswati Sthan are to the east of Bhaktapur one mile off the road to Nagarkot. Both the *Songs* and the *Biography* locate it in Mon; there is no contradiction here as Mon can mean the entire cis-himalayas, but usually if the Kathmandu Valley is indicated then Bal-yul is specified. 'Kurti' may be a corruption of Gurta or Gurda or Gurdaya-ri, but as we have no indication as to this mountains' location that is immaterial. We do know, however, that gNye-bshang means 'intestine' and is the name of the Marsyandi Kola river valley, the land of Nyeshang, where there is a Milarepa cave that is the Manangpa's most sacred power place. There is a cave in Yol-mo, which is close to the Nepal-Tibet border, as mentioned in the Songs, that is also associated with these stories of Mila; and Yol-mo is close enough to the Valley for the King to hear of a well-known yogin meditating there. Nevertheless, we will plump for the Bhaktapur Nyishang Kurti being the authentic Milarepa cave. To add slight weight to that decision, Khyi-ra-pa means not only 'hunter' but also a member of the Kirati tribe (see Das : 100), a people that dominated the Valley from their city south-east of Bhaktapur and east of Panauti in the pre-Licchavi era and thereafter became scattered throughout the Valley and the area to the east of it. Although Hasa Vajra is less well-known than the Indian siddhas, even today his songs are said to be known by some vajracaryas.

48. CANDISWARI

Ekajati: Cantishwari: this shrine is in visual range of Banepa. Ekajati and Devi Candika have one essence.

Candesvari or Candika is a form of Durga or Gauri, the Consort of Siva; she is one of the astamatrka and the navadurga. A composite form of Durga, she is young, beautiful, seductive yet angry, depicted with various number of arms to destroy her demonic offspring, the Asuras, and particularly the buffalo demon, Mahisasura. As the slayer of the buffalo demon she is called Mahisasuramardini. Her temple is located a mile north east of Banepa.

49. NAMO BUDDHA

sTag-mo lus-sbyin (Takmo Lujin, Tigress Body-Gift): Namo Buddha (Homage to the Buddha!): at this power place the King Mahasattva (sNyings-stobs chen-po) gave his body to a tigress. His reliquary-stupa remained underground until the Bhagavan (Sakyamuni) clapped his hands, and miraculously the stupa spontaneously appeared.

"At a place as much as a days walk to the east of Bhaktapur is a stupa that is said to enshrine the remains of the Tathagata Sakyamuni when on the Path of Learning he gave his body to a tigeress." (bLa-ma bTsan-po)

"We need to examine more deeply the validity of sTag-mo lus-sbyin's claim to be the actual place that is mentioned in the Jataka Stories (the ancient legends of Sakyamuni's previous births). If we are to believe in popular fable, the stupa here enshrines the bones and hair of the Bodhisattva who, when practising the deeds of a Bodhisattva (the Six Paramitas, giving, etc.), was moved to such pity at seeing a tigress ravaged by hunger about to devour a small boy, who she had been stalking, that he sacrificed his body to her. In this place there is such fear of the tiger that the people will not utter the real name of the stupa, and since to speak the name of the Buddha is to be free from fear, and since the notions of the Hindus and Buddhists are the same, the Nepalis call this place Namo Buddhaya! If you ask for directions to the Stupa, the local people will not understand you if you ask for Takmo Lujin; you must ask for Namo Buddhaya." (Chos-kyi Nyi-ma)

Namo Buddha is one of the principal places of pilgrimage for the Tibetans south of the Himals. The Newars pay it little attention, but the Bhotiyas worship there in large numbers during the pilgrimage season. bLa-ma bTsan-po states categorically that this is not the stupa relating to the story of the Buddha's sacrifice of his body as told in the gSer-'od dam-pa'i mdo, the Suvarnaprabhasottama Sutra (J. Nobel, Das Goldglanz Sutra, Erster Band, Leiden 1944).

50. RISHISWARA

Chu-mig byang-chub-la (the Spring of Wisdom): Rishiswara: this spring is on the path to India. Upon auspicious days of worship in the first month of the year, you can see a naturally formed image of the Guru in a rock.

"At a place one days march to the southwest is the Spring of the Ambrosia of Wisdom (Chu-mig byang-chub bdud-rtsi)." (Shing-kun dkar-chag)

This power place is a short walk from the main Kathmandu-Raxaul road close to the top of the watershed ridge of the Sivaliks.

In the Vulture Peak Monastery (Bya-rgod phung-po'i dgon-pa) of Kimdol (sKyim-grol), the Newari Bhiksu Vagindra Bajra or Ngag-dbang rDo-rje nas (?) printed these new blocks (of the Guide to the Power Places of Nepal, Bal-yul gnas-yig) on the auspicious 14th day of the month of Saga Dawa in the wood-horse year (1774 A.D.).

Appendix 1

Synopsis of the Gosrnga Vyakarana Sutra?

Arya Gosrnga Vyakarana Mahayana Sutra: `Phags-pa glang-ru lung-bstan zhes-bya-ba theg-pa chen-po'i mdo.

Homage to the Bhagavan Manjusri Kumarabhuta!

Thus have I heard at one time: the god of gods, the Buddha Sakyamuni, after three innumerable kalpas, through the maturation of his accumulated merit, attained complete and perfect Buddhahood. After he had evolved the beings who assembled in other areas of the lands of Jambudvipa, in the palace of Muni Maharishi in the vicinity of Vaisali, [Bodhisattvas, Sravakas, Nagas, Raksasas, Gandharvas, Kinaras, Kings and their subjects] on one occasion gathered. Then at that time, the god of gods, Sakyamuni Buddha, visualised the land of Kusala (dGe-ba) in a future time and brought that vision into reality. Then he addressed the vast assembly, 'Noble Sons, in the north, on the banks of the River Goma, which is near the Ri glang-ru (The Ox-Horn Mountain) is what is known as the Muni Maharishi Palace, the Stupa Goma Salagandha. Verily, in that place there is essential work to be done, and the time is propitious to go there.' Then, at that time, the god of gods the Buddha Sakyamuni and his vast retinue, arose into the sky... and departed for the Ox-Horn Mountain.

Arriving in Khotan on the Ox-Horn mountain, the Buddha looks north and sees a vast lake stretching into the distance. Then taking his throne on Ox-Horn Mountain he looks west and sees the Buddha's palace, the Goma Salagandha Stupa. The Buddha, the Bodhisattvas and arhats then bless the Land of Khotan and pray for the establishment of many monasteries, a rich land, a religious people etc., praying to be reborn there in the future to fulfil their own wishes.

Then in an instant, from within the great lake, 350 lotuses arose, and on top of each lotus was an effulgent image of a Buddha and Bodhisattva. The Buddha explains that in the future a vihara will be established wherever one of these lotuses bloomed.

In answer to the question of who will establish this paradise, the Buddha predicts that a Chinese King will have 1001 sons, all of whom will leave home and establish kingdoms. The youngest son will be sent by his father to Khotan to establish a righteous government in that land. The country will be populated by Indians from the west.

Most of the Sutra is concerned with the Buddha's predictions of the vicissitudes of the dharma in Khotan, its rise and fall, the importance of the Goma Salagandha Stupa and the Kasyapa Stupa and of the Gosrnga Vyakarana Sutra as a panacea for all misfortune, war, poverty, famine, etc. And, also, a large portion is concerned with directions for the religious life, and how the country will be protected from outside threat, from the Chinese and Tibetan armies.

Then at the end, The Buddha spoke to Sariputra and Vaisravana, 'Noble sons, you both go and empty this great lake. Draining it into the River Gyi-sho in the north, do not harm any living creature existing in the water, and reveal the area of this land.' Then Mahasravaka Sariputra and Vaisravana, having asked permission to leave, through their magical power they set out in the sky for the Mountain Sha-ri (Flesh Mountain). Sariputra wielding a monk's staff and Vaisravana wielding a spear, half (phyed-stam?) of the mountain was moved and deposited in the east, so that a vast dried up lake bed was created, the lake together with the living creatures existing in it draining into the Gyi-sho River. In this way Khotan was revealed together with the Goma Salagandha Stupa and the Ox-Horn Mountain.'

The Sutra ends with the divine hosts again blessing the land and its future inhabitants, and finally, praising the Buddha.

References and Bibliography

References

Shing-kun dkar-chag (The Swayambu Chronicles) by Nas-lung Ngag-dbang rDo-rje

Chos-kyi Nyima: *Bal-po'i gnas-kyi dkar-chag*

bLa-ma bTsan-po: *'Dzam-gling rgyas-bshad*; tr. T. Wylie *(A Tibetan Religious Geography of Nepal)*

Blue Annals; tr. G. Roerich

Orgyan mChog-'gyur gLing-pa: *gter-ston* of *Orgyan rnam-thar dpag-bsam ljong-shing*; tr. k. Dowman *(The Legend of the Great Stupa)*

Dharmaswamin: *Chag-lotsawa rnam-thar*; tr. G. Roerich *(The Biography of Dharmaswamin)*

Douglas and White: *Karmapa, the Black Hat Lama of Tibet*

John Locke: *Karunamaya*

Michael Allen: *The Cult of Kumari*

Mila mGur-bum; tr. G.C. Chang *(The Hundred Thousand Songs of Milarepa)*

Nyi-ma 'Od-zer: *gter-ston* of *Guru rnam-thar zangs-gling-ma*

Sakya bzang-po: *gter-ston* of *Bya-rung kha-shor lo-rgyus*; tr. k. Dowman *(The Legend of the Great Stupa)*

sTag-sham Nus-ldan rDo-rje: *gter-ston* of *mTsho-rgyal rnam-thar*

gTsang-myon: *Mila rnam-thar*; tr.L. Lhalungpa *(The Life of Milarepa)*

Urgyan gLing-pa: *gter-ston* of *padma bka'-thang shel-brag-ma*; tr. G-C Toussaint *(Le Dit de Padma)*

Wright Daniel Wright: *History of Nepal*

Wylie Turrell Wylie: *A Tibetan Religious Geography of Nepal*

Regmi D.R.: *Ancient Nepal*

Alaka Chattopadhyaya: *Astisa and Tibet*, Delhi 1981

Tibetan Sources

Bal-po Ngag-dbang rDorje, *Bal-yul gnas-yig*, printed in transliteration Turrel Wylie (1970) *A Tibetan Religious Geography of Nepal*, Rome

Chos-kyi Nyi-ma, 'Yul-chen-po nye-ba'I tshandola bal-po'I gnas-kyi dkar-chag' in A.W Macdonald (ed.) *Kailash* III – 2, (1975)

Dudjom Rinpoche (1967), *'rNying-ma'I chos-'byung'*, Kalimpong

Dudjom Rinpoche, *'Pad-'byung rnam-thar yid-kyi mun-sel'*, Kalimpong

Mani bKa'-bum

Nas-lung Ngag-dbang rDo-rje, '*Bal-yul mchod-rten 'phays-pa shing-kun dang de'I gnas gzhan-rnams-kyi dkar-chag* printed in transliteration in Turrel Wylie (1970) *A Tibetan Religious Geography of Nepal*, Rome

Nyang-ral Nyima 'Od-zer (gter-ston), '*Guru rnam-thar zings-gling-ma*' Handwritten manuscript.

Padma dkar-po *Chos-'byang bstan-pa'I padma rgyas-pa'I nyin-byed* Lokesh Chandra Sata-Pitaka Series 75 1968, New Delhi

'Phas-pa glang-ru lung-bstan-gyi mdo: Arya Gosrnga Vtakarana Mahayana Sutra

Rwa Ye-shes Senge, *Rwa Lotsawa rDo-rje grags-pa'I rnam-thar*, New Delhi

bSod-rnams rGyal-mtshan, *rGyal-rab gsal-ba'i me-long*, Sikkim

sTag-sham Nus-ldan rDo-rje (gter-ston), '*Jo-mo Ye-shemTsho-rgyal rnam-thar*', Bhutanese edition.

Urgyan gLing-pa: gter-ston '*Padma bka'-thang shel-brag-ma*' Dunjom Rinpoche, Benares

Tibetan Translations

Chang, Garma C. (1962) '*The Hundred Thousand Songs of Milarepa*', New York

Dowman, K.C. (1973) *'The Legend of the Great Stupa* (translation of *Bya-rung kha*

shor lo-rgyus gter-ston Sakya-bzang-po and *Orgyan Guru rnam-thar dpag-bsam ljong-shing* by gter-ston Orgyan mChog-'gyur gLing-pa) Emeryville

Lhanllungpa, Lobzang P. (1977) *'The Life of Milarepa'* (Mi-la rnam-thar), New York

Roerich, G (1959) *'The Blue Annals (sDeb-ther sngon-po* by *'Gos lotsawa)*, Calcutta

Roerich, G (1959) *'The Biography of Dharmaswamin"*, Patna

Toussaent, G-C (1978) *'Le Dict de Padma'* (Padma bka'-thang shel-brag-ma) English translation: 'The Life and Liberation of Padmasambhava' tr. Douglas, K. & Bais, G. (1978) Emeryville

Turrel Wylie (1970) *A Tibetan Religious Geography of Nepal*, Rome

Other Sources

Allen, Michael (1975) *'The Cult of Kumari'*, KathmanduChos-' phel, Gedun (1978) *'The White Annals (Deb-ther dkar-po)'* Dharamsala,.

Douglas, N and White, M, (1976) *'Karmapa, the Black Hat Lama of Tibet'*, London

Locke, John, (1980) '*Karunamaya*', Kathmandu

Macdonald, A.W., and Stahl, Anne Vergati, (1979)

'Newar Art' New Delhi

Mana Bajra Bajracarya (tr.) and Smith, Warren, (ed.), (1978) *'A Mythological History of the Nepal Valley from the Swayambhu Purana'* Kathmandu

Pal, P, (1970) *'Vaisnava Iconology in Nepal*